We Were Soldiers
—THE SCREENPLAY—

Randall Wallace

———————————————————————
THE WHEELHOUSE™ SCREENPLAY SERIES

THE WHEELHOUSE™ SCREENPLAY SERIES
Wheelhouse Books, Inc.

Compilation, design, scene notes, correspondence and author interview
©2002 by Wheelhouse Books. All rights reserved.

Screenplay, storyboards and film stills except as indicated otherwise,
©2002 Icon Finance, LLC.
All rights reserved.

This book may not be reproduced, in whole or in part, in any form,
without written permission.

Companies, professional groups, clubs, and other organizations
may qualify for special terms when ordering quantities of this title.
For information, fax: Special Sales - Wheelhouse Books, (818) 907-0819

Editors: Danielle Lemmon and Stephen Zapotoczny
Contributing editors: Jill Rytie and Jason Tracey
Layout design: Gwen Henson
Cover design: Peri Poloni
Storyboards drawn by John Mann and Dan Sweetman

Manufactured in the United States of America.
First Edition

Library of Congress Cataloging-in-Publication Data
Library of Congress PCN: 2002101072
ISBN 0-9712433-2-8

CONTENTS

INTRODUCTION BY LT. GEN. HAROLD G. MOORE (RET.) vii

FOREWORD BY JOSEPH L. GALLOWAY xi

SCREENPLAY KEY xiii

WE WERE SOLDIERS SCREENPLAY 1

SCREENPLAY NOTES AND CHANGES 119

STORYBOARDS 151

CORRESPONDENCE 171

STILLS 183

A CONVERSATION WITH RANDALL WALLACE 191

Lt. General Hal Moore, Ret. and Randall Wallace on the set of *We Were Soldiers*.

INTRODUCTION

BY

LT. GEN. HAROLD G. MOORE (RET.)

The month is June of the year 2000. The heat and humidity in Georgia and Florida are in the miserable high 90's.

Who is that middle-aged guy up to his chest in that muddy Florida swamp water at midnight holding his rifle over his head—and grinning? Then, free-climbing a 100 foot cliff? Who is that lean six footer—the old guy in Army camo, Army boots, G.I. haircut, completing a five mile run in the front ranks of a military formation with 18-25 year-old soldiers in the pre-dawn gray dampness at Fort Benning, Georgia?

It's Hollywood director/screenwriter Randall Wallace. Why is he enduring the tough, demanding, near-torturous Army Ranger School? Here's why: he is preparing to produce a movie on the first major battle of the Vietnam War between American and North Vietnamese Army Regulars; and he is fiercely determined to "get it right."

Many years ago Joe Galloway and I shook hands to write the story of the great American soldiers and the very tough, well-trained North Vietnamese enemy who fought the savage battles in the Ia Drang Valley of Vietnam in November 1965. That was our dream, our goal. We achieved it in 1992 when our book *We Were Soldiers Once... And Young* was published. We hoped our book would provide a better understanding of, and proper honor and respect for, the Americans who served in that tragic war and for the survivors of those who were killed. We wanted to show clearly the stark truth that soldiers in battle fight, kill, and die primarily for each other. From that theme came the principal message of our book—"Hate war, but love the American Warrior."

Shortly after our book was published, we were contacted by many Hollywood filmmakers who wanted to turn our story into a movie—but Joe and I were not comfortable with their proposals.

Then Randall Wallace showed up. He was greatly moved by our book, and very sincere in wanting to share its theme and message with the world on the silver screen.

It may well have been fated that we three would come together to tell this story. Ever since we left the Ia Drang Valley in 1965, Joe and I dreamed of writing our book. Ever since Randall Wallace read that book in the early '90's, he dreamed of putting it on film. Now we all have realized those dreams.

I've known Randall Wallace now for eight or so years. We've conversed many times on the book, his screenplay, and scenes in the movie. He's visited and talked at length with many of the officers and men who fought in the Ia Drang Valley.

My wife and I watched some of the filming and were very impressed by the determination of the cast and crew, from Randy on down, to "get it right." We viewed a rough cut of the film in October before final post-production on sound, music, etc. From what we saw, HE GOT IT RIGHT and has honored all Vietnam veterans—most especially the riflemen, the NCO's and the junior officers down in the ranks where battles are won or lost.

Joe Galloway and his film counterpart, Barry Pepper, on the set of *We Were Soldiers*.

FOREWORD

BY

JOSEPH L. GALLOWAY

This screenplay for Randall Wallace's *We Were Soldiers* was eight years in the making and for all of us it was a labor of love. It was in the fall of 1993 and Hal Moore and I were at Virginia Military Institute for a lecture when we received a phone call from Mr. Wallace.

He had read our book, *We Were Soldiers Once…and Young,* he said, and he loved the story and wanted to make that story into a movie. I told him he had to correctly answer one question before there could be any further discussion: "Do you believe in heroes?" I asked. His immediate reply: "I do. I really do. I just finished a movie called *Braveheart* and if you see it you will know what I believe in."

Hal and I had listened to a lot of pitches and a lot of Hollywood bull, but we decided that Mr. Wallace just might turn out to be a different breed. So we threw in with him. We have never regretted doing so, even though the process of getting from a book to a movie proved to be long and arduous.

At Randall's request, I sat down and wrote my life story, with heavy emphasis on my years as a war correspondent in Vietnam, but also with due attention to where and who I came from. Bits about my Civil War great-grandfathers, and where I came from—"Refugio, Texas, Sir!" turned up in the screenplay.

During five years time the screenplay went through a dozen rewrites. Each time Hal and I read, commented, offered suggestions, suggested corrections. Each version, from first to final, never failed to bring tears to our eyes. The power of a great screenplay is little short of magical. Although much disappears in turning a 412-page work of military history into a 120-page, triple-spaced, screenplay—the gifted screenwriter adds back magic, line by line.

Randall later told us what made him pick up the phone and track us down in 1993. It was a line in the Prologue to our book: "Hollywood got it wrong every damned time, whetting twisted political knives on the bones of our dead brothers." For him it was so in his face—a challenge that he would strive to meet. "I want to get Vietnam right this one time," he told me. "It may not be all fact, but it should all be the truth."

For 36 long years Hal Moore and I have been devoted to telling the story of this overlooked battle, these unnoticed men, this orphaned and abandoned war. Our quest consumed ten years of research, a year of writing and editing, three trips back to Vietnam. Randall Wallace quietly joined us in our obsession, in our passion, for this story.

For once, this once, Hollywood got Vietnam right.

Thanks for your dedication and friendship, Randall.

Garry Owen, Sir!

SCREENPLAY KEY

Reading a screenplay is like reading other types of literature, with a few exceptions. This key has been included to make reading this screenplay a little easier.

2. SCENE HEADING

1. TRANSITION — Cut to:

3. SCENE NUMBER

85 EXT. AT THE CUT-OFF PLATOON - DAY   85

Bullets zing around Charlie Lose, the only Medic among the seventeen men cut off on the isolated mound, who is kneeling above Herrick and shoving compresses into his huge wounds.

                HERRICK
    Savage...Don't let 'em get the signals
    codes. ...I'm glad I could die for my
    country.

4. SCENE DESCRIPTION

He dies. Medic Lose closes his Lieutenant's eyes. Bungum is crying, lying next to Palmer; then he hears -

                PALMER

5. CHARACTER

    Bungum...

6. DIALOGUE

                BUNGUM
            (brightening)
    Sarge!

7. PARENTHETICAL

                PALMER
    ...Tell my wife I love her.

---

1. **Transition:** *A word or phrase placed at the beginning or end of a scene that describes the way scenes move from one to the other. FADE OUT, CUT TO:, DISSOLVE TO: AND SMASH TO:*
2. **Scene Heading:** *A description found at the beginning of most scenes that tells whether the scene takes place on the interior or exterior (INT. OR EXT.), in what locale (ex. MOORE'S LIVING ROOM, NORTH VIETNAMESE BUNKER, etc.), and what time of day (ex. DAY, NIGHT, EVENING, LATER, etc.).*
3. **Scene Number:** *The number listed on the right and left margins next to each scene heading.*
4. **Scene Description:** *Where action, characters, or locations are described.*
5. **Character:** *The name of the person who is speaking.*
6. **Dialogue:** *The lines the character is speaking.*
7. **Parenthetical:** *A short description of what a character is feeling or doing when speaking.*

WE WERE SOLDIERS

Screenplay by Randall Wallace

Based on the book
We Were Soldiers Once... And Young
by
Lt. General Harold G. Moore (Ret.)
and Joseph L. Galloway

Final Shooting Script

Out of BLACK...

> **VOICE**
> These are the true events of November, 1965, in the Ia Drang Valley of Vietnam, a place our country does not remember, in a war it does not understand. This story is a testament to the young Americans who died in the Valley of Death, and a tribute to the young men of the People's Army of Vietnam who died by our hand in that place.
> (beat)
> To tell this story, I must start at the beginning.

1   EXT. A HOT, DRY ROAD - HIGHLANDS OF VIETNAM - DAY   1

SOLDIERS, IN BATTLE ATTIRE move along the road. They are crack troops, hardened and scarred by battle; a double column of men, moving side by side, watching the grass and trees on the flanks of the road.

> **VOICE OVER**
> But where does it begin? Maybe in June of 1954, when French Group Mobile 100 moved into the same Central Highlands of Vietnam, where we would go eleven years later.

The soldiers are speaking French. A CAPTAIN and LIEUTENANT, both wearing DeGaulle-style caps, confer-- their words subtitled...

> **FRENCH CAPTAIN**
> See anything?

> **FRENCH LIEUTENANT**
> No, Captain.

The Captain wipes sweat from his stinging eyes.

> **FRENCH CAPTAIN**
> Fucking grass. Fucking heat. Fucking country--

As he rises to wave his men forward, a bullet slaps through the peak of his cap, splashing brain blood over the Lieutenant. Springing a classic ambush from the tall grass on the right side of the Vietminh. Command-detonated land mines explode in the roadway, throwing men into the air and blocking the French vehicles.

                        FRENCH LIEUTENANT
                   Sound the rally call!

The bugler behind him starts to blow the battle notes, but a
bullet pierces his neck. The first crash of rifle fire and
grenades tears into the French ranks, but they are a potent
fighting force, more than two hundred battle-hardened
veterans. They return fire immediately.

Then the Vietminh spring the other jaw of their trap; a
second force rises behind the French and sprays them with
automatic weapons fire. Vietminh snipers, roped into the
tree tops, pour pinpoint rifle fire onto the road, killing
the officers. A mass of Vietminh troops charge from the
hills flanking the road. The French fight back; the
Lieutenant leads gallantly, directing a machine gun that
kills many of the charging enemy; his men are bravely
standing their ground, killing the Vietminh who ferociously
race into their ranks, shooting, stabbing, slinging grenades.
For a moment, the battle is in doubt.

Among the Vietminh is a young officer named AHN. He crouches
as the bullets from the French gun crash into the trees
around him and tear through his comrades. Some of them
shrink back from its fire. Ahn's eyes take on a strange
stillness; he fixes a bayonet onto the end of his rifle, and
charges.

We follow his charge, through the trees, past the hand-to-
hand fighting at the edges of the road, through the smoke and
noise, right to the Lieutenant; Ahn buries his bayonet into
the Frenchman, shoots the gunners, and waves his soldiers
forward. The fight is all but over.

A VIETMINH SERGEANT moves up beside Ahn; the young bugler is
bleeding at their feet, his mouth moving soundlessly.

                        VIETMINH SERGEANT
                     (Vietnamese, subtitles)
                   Do we take prisoners?

                             AHN
                   No. Kill all they send, and they will
                   stop coming.

The sergeant shoots the bugler, then moves on. Ahn spots the
French bugle; he lifts it from the bugler's dead hand, then
calls to one of his men, who has just fired a heart shot into
a wounded Frenchman.

As the soldier looks up Ahn tosses him the bugle, then looks out over the fields of fire, where all along the road his men complete the massacre of their enemies. Ahn's eyes are distant, as if he can see into the future.

DISSOLVE TO:

2   EXT. A CLEAR BLUE SKY - DAY   2

A U.S. Army transport plane cuts its way through the air, over an American landscape.

SUPERIMPOSE:

           Ft. Bragg, North Carolina   1962

3   DOWN ON THE GROUND, observers sit in a cluster of jeeps in an   3
open field. One of the observers is GENERAL HARRY KINNARD. He and the others are watching THROUGH BINOCULARS. The JUMP COORDINATOR has a field radio.

                    JUMP COORDINATOR
        Here they come.
          (into radio)
        We have you on visual. Confirm shortened
        pull time.

4   EXT. THE PLANE - DAY   4

In its open side door stands a lean officer; he is HAL MOORE. He's wearing a helmet and parachute gear; he holds a radio.

                JUMP COORDINATOR (RADIO VOICE)
        Hang onto your rip cord, we're running
        short of 'em.

                    MOORE
        Roger that.

He hands the radio to an air crewman and calmly steps out into the rush of air.

The chute snaps open too quickly; Moore's body jerks like a rag doll as wind catches the parachute silk and snatches it straight back into the huge tail section of the plane.

Suddenly Moore is being dragged along at 150 miles an hour. The earth and the sky are spinning wildly for him, his chute a mess of torn silk and fouled lines.

5   INSIDE THE PLANE the crew reacts by hitting emergency   5
buttons; but there's nothing in the world anyone can do to save Moore.

6   DOWN ON THE GROUND, THE OBSERVERS see the emergency.   6

                    JUMP COORDINATOR
            He's hung on the tail! Maybe if he
            deploys his backup it'll tear him free!

                    GENERAL KINNARD
            At 150 miles an hour it'll rip his body
            in two.

    Moore's a dead man; everybody on the ground knows it.

7   HANGING ON THE PLANE'S TAIL SECTION, AT 150 M.P.H.   7

    In solitary, personal danger, Moore keeps his head; he grips
    the lines and pulls himself into the fierce wind, then lets
    go and the lines snap taut, but don't release. He does it
    again. Nothing. He tugs and snaps on a single side of the
    line...and the whole tangled mess breaks free.

8   Now he's tumbling to earth with his main chute streaming; if   8
    he pulls his reserve and it tangles in the main lines, he's
    dead. The earth rushes toward him at sickening speed...

9   ON THE GROUND, KINNARD and the others watch Moore plummeting   9
    to his death...

10 MOORE draws a switchblade from his boot, cuts the fouled   10
    lines away, and pulls the cord of his reserve. His body
    falls INTO CAMERA as the GROUND'S POV, when suddenly his
    chute pops opens, and he settles to earth.

11 He stays on his feet, landing in an easy trot, towing in the   11
    reserve chute and taking off the helmet as the jeeps and
    ambulances of Ft. Bragg come screaming up to him. He salutes
    the General, hands something to the Jump Coordinator, and
    walks casually to a seat in another jeep.

                    MOORE
            We're gonna have to lengthen the pull
            time.

    The Jump Coordinator looks down at the two ripcords, and
    can't believe Moore remembered. General Kinnard shakes his
    head and smiles.

12 EXT. PENTAGON - DAY   12

    Over an establishing shot of the Pentagon, we hear the voice
    of a GENERAL.

                    GENERAL (V.O.)
            Southeast Asia is heating up...

13 INT. PENTAGON CORRIDOR - DAY   13

    Kinnard and another GENERAL walk down the corridor.

                        GENERAL
              The White House anticipates a build up,
              and wants a victory--over cavemen, in
              black pajamas.

                        GENERAL KINNARD
              We wouldn't be there if they hadn't
              already beaten the French Army.

                        GENERAL
              The French Army? What's that?
                   (beat)
              The problem in Vietnam is terrain.
              Jungle, mountains, rivers--manuever is a
              nightmare. So we've come up with a plan
              to use helicopters. Leap in and out of
              battle. They want you to run the test on
              this idea.

    Kinnard nods; he welcomes the challenge.

                        GENERAL KINNARD
              It'll take a hell of a combat leader.
              I know a young light Colonel named Hal
              Moore. He led a combat company in Korea.
              After that he volunteered to test
              experimental parachutes.

                        GENERAL
              Experimental parachutes?
                   (beat)
              Sounds like just the guy.

14 EXT. TWO-LANE GEORGIA HIGHWAY, 1964 - DAY   14

    Hal Moore drives a station wagon packed with kids and stuffed
    animals, and towing a U-Haul trailer, along a Georgia
    highway. Next to him is JULIE, his warm, beautiful wife.
    The kids--five of them--are singing in the back.

15 EXT. FRONT GATE, FT. BENNING, GEORGIA - DAY   15

    Hal stops at the front gate of the military base and hands
    over his papers; the guards salute and raise the barricade.

    As they pass the guard, one of Hal and Julie's boys salutes
    back to the guard, while CECILE, his five-year-old daughter,
    makes a funny face at him.

16   EXT. FT. BENNING - DAY   16

The car and U-Haul pass the Ft. Benning jump towers, busy with paratrooper practice. Hal turns into the section of the fort where soldiers' families are provided housing. They stop before a house on a tree-lined street, and the children hop out, excited. Hal watches Julie for her reaction; she turns and smiles at him; she approves.

CLOSE - COMBAT BOOTS - DAY

Cecile wears Moore's combat boots, clomping to the house as she helps her siblings and parents unload the trailer. Hal and Julie see her and smile at each other.

ANGLE - DOWN THE STREET

Two other families are moving in down the street, carrying boxes in from their cars. The fathers are in civilian clothes but have buzz cuts; they are CAPTAIN BOB EDWARDS and CAPTAIN TOM METSKER, both in their late twenties. They wave to Moore, then stop to confer.

                    EDWARDS
          How much you know about our new Colonel?

                    METSKER
          He was in Korea. Has a Masters in
          International Relations from Harvard.

CATHERINE, Metsker's wife, kisses his cheek as she moves by with their daughter, 2-year-old KAREN.

                    CATHERINE
          Get to work.

Edwards looks down the block and sees Moore carrying a massive stack of books into his house. The top volume is "History of Cavalry Battles".

                    EDWARDS
          Harvard? He's not one of those academic
          pussies, is he?

                    METSKER
          Hal Moore?

Metsker laughs.

                    METSKER (cont'd)
          He led a combat unit in Korea. After
          that he tested experimental parachutes.

                    EDWARDS
          Experimental parachutes? The kind where
          you're not sure if they're gonna work?

AT MOORE'S FRONT DOOR, Moore emerges from his house he sees a
flight of helicopters blast overhead in a training run,
clipping the treetops. Moore's eyes grab the lead chopper.

17   EXT. FORT BENNING - POV HELICOPTER - DAY   17

     Speeding helicopters rush over the hot sandy ground of Ft.
     Benning. The pilot is BRUCE CRANDALL, a handsome Major in
     his late 20's. Stenciled on his helmet is his nickname:
     SNAKESHIT. From his perspective in the lead chopper we see
     the vastness of the base: rows of barracks, the parade
     grounds, the endless tracts of training areas.

                    CRANDALL
          Takin' 'em lower, Too Tall!

     ED "TOO TALL TO FLY" FREEMAN, the gawky 6'8" pilot in the
     chopper on his right side radios back--

                    TOO TALL
          Lower, Snake? I'm already getting a pine
          tree suppository.

     They swoop low, barely over the scrub trees of Ft. Benning.

18   EXT. FT. BENNING - GUNNERY RANGE - DAY   18

     Dirty and sweaty, RUSSELL ADAMS and BILL BECK are a machine
     gun team; Adams is stocky with powerful arms, Beck is lanky.
     Adams fires the M-60 at a target, demolishing it. A WHISTLE
     sounds the end of gunnery training. A huge pile of shell
     casings shows how much they've practiced.

                    VOICE
          Fall out!

                    BECK
          Finally. Whatta ya wanna do tonight?

                    ADAMS
          Let's find some girls and go shootin'.

19   EXT. FT. BENNING - HELICOPTER LANDING AREA - DAY   19

     Chopper crews and mechanics playing a game of baseball--
     except that the ball is a burned-out sparkplug and the bat a
     greasy suspension rod;

the batter is Crandall, wearing his helmet with the eyeshield down, and "SNAKESHIT" painted above it. The game is improvised, something to make more enjoyable the business of helicopter maintenance going on nearby.

                    CRANDALL
         Come on, gimme your best shot!

Too Tall is on the mound. He goes into exaggerated windup contortions, then fires the plug at Crandall. Crandall swings, driving the plug out into the dust among the scrambling outfielders, leaving the spectators--more of his ground crews--to cheer him. Crandall pops open his visor and starts circling the bases, strut-running backwards, doing his own announcing to the delight of his audience.

                    CRANDALL (cont'd)
         Snakeshit drives that one to the moon,
         sportsfans! To the moon!

The outfielders tumble and dive and fight over the sparkplug; one of them comes up with it and pegs it to a cut-off man, who fires it toward home.

Crandall has dawdled enough to make it close; now as the relay comes in, he turns to run...

It's close; a hand catches the plug, as Crandall slides under the tag...

                    CRANDALL (cont'd)
         Safe!

                    TOO TALL
         Out!

                    CRANDALL
         Bullshit, I was--

He sees two mirror polished jump boots, and looks up to see the chiseled form of Hal Moore, who has put the tag on him. Crandall gets to his feet, saluting. Moore rises and finds himself eye level with the chest of Too Tall.

                    MOORE
         You're a pilot?

                    TOO TALL
         Too Tall Freeman, sir. You call, we
         haul.

                    MOORE
         What do you drink, Crandall?

20 Moore pulls two cans of beer from his pocket and hands one
to Crandall, leading him on a walk past a line of helicopters
undergoing maintenance.

>   MOORE (CONT'D)
>   Your men call you... Snakeshit?
>
>   CRANDALL
>   An affectionate appellation of my
>   comrades-in-arms, Sir. 'Cause I fly
>   lower than snakeshit.
>
>   MOORE
>   I have a problem, Snakeshit. And I think
>   you're the solution.
>
>   CRANDALL
>   I been called a lotta things, Colonel,
>   but never a solution.
>
>   MOORE
>   Air Cavalry. You know what that really
>   means? We fly into hostile territory,
>   out-numbered, 10,000 miles from home.
>   The whole battleground may be no bigger
>   than a football field. And if the
>   choppers stop coming, we all get
>   slaughtered.

Moore's given it to him straight; Crandall just stares.

>   MOORE (cont'd)
>   Chopper pilots won't fly into hell for
>   strangers. So when the shooting starts,
>   you're the ones I want supporting us.
>
>   CRANDALL
>   Why us?
>
>   MOORE
>   You guys look like shit, but your
>   equipment is immaculate. Yesterday was
>   Sunday, you didn't have to be training--
>   but you were. And you have pilots like
>   that Too Tall character who are outside
>   the limits of Army regs, but they want to
>   fly with you...for some reason. Seems
>   like they think you're the best.
>
>   CRANDALL
>   That's 'cause I only recruit the dumb
>   ones.

Moore holds up his beer. Crandall grins, and they click cans.

      CRANDALL (cont'd)
 To the Air Cav!

21 EXT. ENLISTED MEN'S SPORT RANGE, FT. BENNING - EVENING 21

Adams, Beck, Ouellette, and WILLIE GODBOLDT, a black private, have gathered on a makeshift range enlisted men use for shooting their own weapons. They're in their civvies now-- blue jeans and T-shirts-- and Adams has even brought a blue-eyed redneck babe. She's brought a pump action shotgun. He fires a shot off into the air over the pond and then carefully hands her the shotgun.

      ADAMS
 You just get comfortable darlin'. I'll
 be right back.

Adams moves to the tailgate of his pickup where Beck is laying out his personal pistols, preparing to shoot. Ouellette has set up a barbeque and is tuning a transistor radio to a country station. Godboldt is rigging his fishing tackle.

      BECK
 You got a girlfriend, Willie?

      GODBOLDT
 I've forgot more about women then I ever
 knew.

      OUELLETTE
 What?

He pulls several other pistols from his satchel to toss onto the table, Beck admires the girl's rear.

      BECK
 Damn, Russell, where'd you find her?

      ADAMS
  (Still dumping guns)
 I ain't never gonna win the Nobel Peace
 Prize. But I'm gonna get pussy.
  (beat)
 'Scuse me boys, I've gotta teach her how
 to hold something long and hard.

Adams grabs a handful of charcoal briquettes from the barbeque walks back over to the girl, and makes a show of helping her position the shotgun.

                              BECK
                    Hey, Ouellette. Whatta ya get when you
                    cross a jackass with an onion?

Ouellette's busy with the radio; it won't tune.

                              OUELLETTE
                    What?

                              BECK
                    Usually you just get a onion with floppy
                    ears. But once in a great while, you get
                    a piece 'a ass that'll bring tears to
                    your eyes.

Adams tosses a charcoal briquette into the air. The girl
fires and hits it. Adams is stunned. He tosses another and
she hits that too. Adams hands her the briquettes and moves
back to his friends.

                              BECK (CONT'D)
                    I think maybe she's done this before,
                    Russell.

Godboldt and Ouellette are laughing.

                              ADAMS
                    She said she hadn't.

                              BECK
                    Yeah, she's a virgin too.

The girl tosses two briquettes at the same time, and breaks
them. Adams is stunned.

                              OUELLETTE
                    Whatta you guys think this new unit's
                    gonna be like?

                              ADAMS
                    It's all up to the Sergeant-Major. If
                    he's easy, it's easy.

                              BECK
                    Then we're shit outta luck, cause I know
                    the new Sergeant-Major. Name's Plumley.

Adams shakes his head gravely.

                              OUELLETTE
                    Plumley..? Sounds like Pansy.

                        BECK
            Let me tell you about Plumley.

All the troopers are listening; this is information that
concerns every moment of an enlisted man's life.

                        BECK (cont'd)
            ...I'd been in six months when they
            assigned me to this Heavy Weapons unit,
            and the Platoon Sergeant is the nastiest
            looking motherfucker I ever saw. All
            scarred up, one bad bastard.

22   IN A QUICK, SUBLIMINAL FLASHBACK, we see Beck in a formation   22
      of enlisted men, and his description of the sergeant is apt.

23   IN THE PRESENT   23

                        BECK (cont'd)
            We had this green lieutenant, fresh outta
            university R.O.T.C...

24   IN FLASHBACK, the new Lieutenant addresses his men with   24
      arrogant self-assurance.

                        BECK (cont'd)
            He tells us he wants us to put on our
            ribbons, whatever we've been awarded, so
            he can see what kinda men he's got.

25   IN THE PRESENT, Adams' girlfriend now picks up a personally-   25
      owned .45 pistol and fires a clip, expertly ejecting it and
      loading another.

                        ADAMS
            She's got brothers.

                        BECK
            She's been datin' a Ranger.

                        OUELLETTE
            What about this sergeant?

                        BECK
            Oh yeah. So we go back and put on our
            stuff, and reassemble. But the Sergeant,
            he didn't put on his ribbons, so the
            Lieutenant chews him out in front of the
            whole unit, orders him to go pin on his
            dress shit.

The girl fires again. Beck looks back.

                    BECK (cont'd)
               In about ten minutes, the sarge comes
               back...

26   FLASHBACK; WE SEE THE ACTION...ON A PARADE GROUND   26

      The arrogant Lieutenant realizes that men are beginning to
      snicker. He turns to see the Sergeant marching up...

      Totally naked. Except for two Medals of Honor around his
      neck.

                    BECK (V.O.) (cont'd)
               Not one Medal of Honor around his neck.
               Two. Besides that, naked as a jaybird.

      The troopers can't help themselves; spasms of laughter
      convulse their ranks. The Sergeant marches straight up to
      the Lieutenant, salutes, and glares at the shamed lieutenant
      until he walks away.

27   PRESENT TIME - EXT. THE FIELDS AT FT. BENNING - DAY   27

      The men are listening raptly to Beck's story. Ouellette
      slaps the transistor radio in frustration, and it tunes right
      in.

                    OUELLETTE
               And that buck naked double Medal of Honor
               winning crazy son-of-a-bitch Sergeant was
               Plumley?

                    BECK
               Naw! That was Sergeant McDoon.

                    OUELLETTE
               Then... what the hell's that story got to
               do with Plumley?

                    BECK
               Because Plumley was McDoon's boss. And
               McDoon? He was scared shitless of
               Plumley.

      This sinks in on all the troopers.

                    OUELLETTE
               Ooo, shiiiit...

28   CLOSE ON A NAME STRIP: PLUMLEY. It's sewn onto the broad   28
      chest of SERGEANT-MAJOR BASIL PLUMLEY, a tall, rawboned West
      Virginian with fierce eyes, eternally watchful, missing
      nothing. As he strides along,

EXT. FT. BENNING TARMAC - DAY

He passes a young Sergeant, ERNIE SAVAGE, a friendly country boy with an Alabama accent.

> SAVAGE
> Good mornin', Sergeant-Major.

Plumley's voice is an ominous growl--

> PLUMLEY
> What the hell you know about what kinda Got-dam day it is?

Plumley leaves Savage shaken and rounds a corner, to see

29 EXT. HANGAR - FT. BENNING - DAY   29

Gathered in a giant hangar are two dozen officers. Edwards and Metsker are among them. They watch a MINI GUN spin, fascinated.

> METSKER
> Four thousand rounds a second.

> EDWARDS
> Hardly a fair fight.

> METSKER
> Ain't no such thing.

Plumley scowls at his watch and barks--

> PLUMLEY
> 'Tension!

The officers snap to attention; Plumley's timing is perfect: around the other corner strides Moore. His officers study him. His waist is narrow, the muscles ropey in his neck and arms; his jump boots are glossy, and well broken in.

> MOORE
> At ease, Gentlemen! Welcome to the new cavalry. We will ride into battle--and this will be our horse.

At that moment a Huey hops over the top of the hangar and plummets to earth, its blades blasting to give the chopper a feather-light touchdown; Crandall, at the controls, salutes and grins from his glass bubble, then skims back skyward. Moore's eyes sweep his officers.

                    MOORE (CONT'D)
          I assure you that neither the new
          technology nor your status as officers
          will keep you above the danger. Sergeant-
          Major Plumley and I come from the
          paratroopers, where the officer is always
          the first one out of the plane--because
          to follow your instincts, and inspire
          your men by your example, you have to be
          with them where the metal meets the meat.

The young officers are riveted; in one moment, they know
their Colonel. Edwards looks at Metsker, and nods; Hal Moore
is a leader.

                    MOORE (cont'd)
          Sgt. Major Plumley made all four combat
          jumps of the 82nd Airborne in World War
          Two: Sicily, Salerno, Normandy, and
          Holland, plus one into Korea.

The young officers look up at Plumley, all 6'2" of him, like
they might look at God.

                    MOORE (cont'd)
          He answers to me and to me alone. I hope
          you like training, gentlemen. Because me
          and the Sergeant Major, we love it.

30   EXT. TRAINING RUN - DAY   30

Moore leads the officers on a training run, in combat boots,
through the stifling heat and marshy ground of Ft. Benning,
lecturing while his officers gasp...

                    MOORE
          Three strikes and you're not out! There
          is always one more thing you can do to
          influence any situation in your favor--
          and when you've done it, there's one more
          thing!...

They splash THROUGH A STREAM; the young officers gasp, but
Moore is jogging backwards, calling in an even voice--

                    MOORE (cont'd)
          A leader will either contaminate his
          environment and his unit with his
          pessimism, or he will inspire confidence.

They struggle up A LONG HILL; Moore calls back--

                    MOORE (cont'd)
               He must exhibit his determination to
               prevail no matter what the odds or how
               desperate the situation...

Moore keeps running; he isn't winded, he doesn't even look
hot. Edwards and Metsker stop for a breather; but they see
Plumley coming up, glaring at them as he sweeps up the
stragglers, and they run on rather than face him. At the top
of the hill...

                    MOORE (cont'd)
               Get some water, gentlemen. You're going
               to need it.

31   CLOSE ON MOORE, IN HIS UNIFORM   31

                    MOORE (cont'd)
               Have you said your prayers?

He looks stern, unyielding; but his eyes are softer than
usual; he's looking at HIS CHILDREN, in the barracks-like
bedroom of their home. The children, already in bed, look at
each other guiltily.

                    MOORE (cont'd)
               Come on, I'll say 'em with you.

He moves to one of the sets of bunk beds, and kneels. His
children, all five of them, kneel beside him, as he crosses
himself; he's a devout Catholic. Julie moves to the doorway
to watch; it's a beautiful moment to her.

                    MOORE (cont'd)
               Hail Mary, full of grace...

His children are repeating the prayer--all except one, his
darling, angelic Cecile, five years old.

                    MOORE (CONT'D)
               Cecile, I don't hear you.

                    CECILE
               I don't want to be a Catholic. I want to
               be a Methodist like Mommy.

Uh-oh, religious rebellion among the ranks.

                    MOORE
               And why is that, honey?

                    CECILE
          So I can pray whatever I want.

Julie nearly swallows her tongue to keep from laughing. Hal
glances at her, then hears his eldest son, thirteen year-old
GREG rebuke Cecile...

                    GREG
          That's a sin.

                    MOORE
          No, God made you hard-headed, it's not a
          sin. Cecile...do you want to thank God
          for our family?

                    CECILE
          Yes sir...

                    MOORE
          Then let's do it. Hail Mary, full of
          grace...

32   INT. MOORE'S BEDROOM - NIGHT   32

Julie is in bed, still holding back laughter as Hal brushes
his teeth in the bathroom.

                    MOORE
          I can feel you laughing, even in here.

                    JULIE
          I'm not laughing, I'm marveling.

                    MOORE
          At what?

                    JULIE
          That you could find stubbornness in our
          children, and think it comes from anybody
          else but you.

He comes in.

                    MOORE
          Yeah? I'll give you something to marvel
          at!

He kisses her, tickles her.

                    JULIE
          Shh! The children!

MOORE
          How do you think we ended up with five?

He kisses her tenderly. Then he pulls back and looks into
her eyes.

                    MOORE (cont'd)
          When I pray whatever I want to--I thank
          God for you.

He kisses her again, tender as the Georgia air.

33   EXT. TREE-LINED STREET - FT. BENNING - MORNING   33

Ernie Savage is walking down the street; his steps falter as
he sees Plumley coming. Resolving not to be intimidated,
Savage perks up and speaks.

                    SAVAGE
          Beautiful morning, Sergeant-Major!

                    PLUMLEY
          So you're a fuckin' weatherman now?

Plumley strides on, to the front of the Moore home. Moore
emerges from his house to find Plumley waiting there for him
with two styrofoam cups of coffee. He hands one to Moore.
They start off together. Moore yawns; Plumley gives him a
sideways look. Moore takes a sip of coffee; it's super
strong.

                    PLUMLEY (cont'd)
          Made it myself, last Wednesday.

They pass two new arrivals, carrying personal items into one
of the officer's houses; they are LT. JACK GEOGHEGAN and his
wife BARBARA. Jack is bright-eyed, slender, handsome;
Barbara is a dark-haired, blue-eyed beauty, very pregnant.

                    PLUMLEY (cont'd)
          They've sent us some new officers. Real
          green. Want us to train 'em up.

                    MOORE
          Must be starting another unit.

                    PLUMLEY
          Sent new rifles too, the M-16.

                    MOORE
          Supposed to be a great weapon.

                    PLUMLEY
          Lotsa plastic. Feels like a b-b gun to
          me. I'll stick with my pistol.

He taps the .45 he carries. Moore smiles.

                    MOORE
          You think we're gonna be close enough to
          the enemy to use that?

                    PLUMLEY
          Whatta you think, Sir?

34   EXT. FT. BENNING SWAMPS - DAY   34

Metsker is training four enlisted men to use the new PRC-25
field radio; Ouellette is among them. Ouellette uses his
masterful touch to tune in distant voices.

                    RADIO VOICES
          I see something! I have movement.

They hear Moore coming, calling--

                    MOORE'S VOICE
          A leader must remain calm and cool, must
          ignore the explosions, the dust, smoke,
          the screams of wounded, the yells of the
          dying! This is normal on a battlefield!

Moore stops to watch as his officers stagger by; near the
front are two young lieutenants, Jack Geoghegan and the
strong, eager HENRY HERRICK, gasping, getting water. Moore
notices the sounds of screaming and shooting, American
voices, broken, staticky-

                    RADIO VOICES
          Get some artillery on 'em! We need
          ammo!... Medics!!...

Moore moves toward the radio, as all the officers begin to
hear the disturbing sound.

                    MOORE
          Who tuned that in?

Ouellette is afraid to admit he did it.

                    HERRICK
          Where the hell is that coming from?

He looks up and sees forty feet of antenna wire strung
through the trees.

                    METSKER
          It's Vietnam. The new radio's picking
          up atmospheric bounce.

                    RADIO VOICES
          ...fuckers are all over the place!!...

The signal dims out, lost in static. For a moment all is
quiet in the Georgia marshes, the young officers realize
they've just heard the real war. Moore glares at them.

                    MOORE
          When Crazy Horse was a baby, he nursed at
          the breast of every woman in his tribe.
          The Sioux Indians raised their children
          that way.

The troopers all look at each other, mystified at Moore's
purpose in telling them this.

                    MOORE (cont'd)
          Sioux warriors grew up calling every
          woman Mother. Every older warrior they
          called Grandfather.

Even Plumley's scowling. Moore's insistent.

                    MOORE (cont'd)
          They fought as a family.

Now they all get it, though Plumley still frowns.

                    MOORE (cont'd)
          Take care of your men. Teach them to
          take care of each other. Because when
          this starts--

He points to the radio...

                    MOORE (cont'd)
          ...each other is all we're gonna have.

As Moore says this his eyes find his new lieutenants, so
earnest and green. Moore walks away. Plumley lingers,
scowling at the young officers, and growls...

                    PLUMLEY
          Any 'a you sumbitches calls me Grandpaw,
          I'll kill ya.

Plumley strides off, following Moore.

35 CLOSE - JACK GEOGHEGAN, one of those lieutenants, is leading   35
his men through A SWAMP exercise. They are struggling
through water waist deep.

> GEOGHEGAN
> Watch your spacing! Come on!

He's first to the other side, directing his men.

> GEOGHEGAN (cont'd)
> Cover, cover, quick! Stay spread enough
> they can't take us out with one grenade,
> and tight enough we don't get separated!

Half of Geoghegan's platoon is black. Willie Godboldt, is
bringing up the rear. As he makes it to the bank and
collapses, Geoghegan barks like Moore...

> GEOGHEGAN (cont'd)
> We were slow. We've gotta get tighter,
> and tougher. Two miles double-time,
> let's go!

He leads them off on the run.

In the rear of his line, Godboldt is struggling, and three
soldiers--one black and two white--are hassling him.

> BLACK PRIVATE
> Gettin' tired, Willie?

> WHITE PRIVATE
> Hey Godboldt, you boys are built for
> speed but not endurance, huh?

Godboldt says nothing; but Geoghegan, drifting to the rear of
his platoon, has heard the exchange.

AS HIS MEN REACH THE SHADE, and stop...

> GEOGHEGAN
> Everybody, take your boots off!

They don't understand the order, but they obey. Godboldt
hesitates.

> GEOGHEGAN (CONT'D)
> You too, Godboldt!

Godboldt pulls off his boots, and the guys act like his feet
smell worse than anybody's.

                    GEOGHEGAN (cont'd)
               Socks, too.

Godboldt obeys. Then Geoghegan kneels and takes Godboldt's
hot wet feet in his hands, and carefully examines them, in
front of the whole platoon.

                    GEOGHEGAN (cont'd)
               Willie, draw fresh socks from supply, and
               keep your feet dusted with powder.

Geoghegan looks at the men who were hazing Godboldt.

                    GEOGHEGAN (cont'd)
               Everybody! Check each other's feet.

36   INCLUDE - MOORE AND PLUMLEY, watching unseen from the tree   36
     line, through binoculars. They see what Geoghegan's doing.

                    MOORE
               That young man's a leader.

                    PLUMLEY
               That other feller, the big strong one
               there--

He points in another direction at Lt. Herrick running up a
hill, yelling at his struggling men.

                    PLUMLEY (cont'd)
               He wants to win medals.

And in Plumley's mind, that ain't good.

37   INT. FT. BENNING, BASE HOUSING - CHILD'S BEDROOM - NIGHT   37

Hal is sitting by the bedside of his five-year-old daughter,
Cecile, reading to her...

                    HAL
               ..."And the Little Star said, '"I just
               want to shine, as brightly as I can for
               as long as I can...'"

He sees that she's asleep. He kisses her cheek.

38   IN THE HALLWAY   38

Hal looks in on the boys, touching the hair of each with his
lips. He stops at the doorway and glances back at them.
Something stops him there; he stares at his sons for an extra
beat, and then moves on to his own bedroom.

39 INT. MOORE'S BEDROOM - NIGHT   39

Julie lies drowsy and beautiful in her nightgown. She stirs as Hal lies down next to her.

>   JULIE
> I was thinking of starting a group for the wives. Think that's a good idea?

>   HAL
> Hm?... Yeah, sure.

She presses her back to him, and pulls his arm around her.

40 INT. MOORE'S BEDROOM - NIGHT - LATER   40

Julie rolls over in her sleep, reaching for Hal. But he isn't there, and she wakes. The clock says 3:45.

41 INT. MOORE HOUSE - KITCHEN - NIGHT   41

Hal is sitting at the kitchen table behind a stack of books: "History of the Vietnamese People," "The Wars of Indochina." The book he is currently studying is in French; he reads the text and turns the page to find a photograph of the aftermath of the massacre of French Group Mobile 100, the slaughter we saw earlier.

His eyes lock on the picture: bodies sprawled everywhere, mangled by bullets, bayonets, machetes, young bodies stripped of uniforms and equipment, bare in the sun.

Moore looks up and covers the picture with note paper as Julie shuffles in and kisses his neck.

>   JULIE
> Can't sleep?

>   MOORE
> My men are so young. They've added a new crop, even greener. And when I look at them, I see our boys.

>   JULIE
> Then you're just the man to lead them.

She strokes his hair and hugs him, trying to give him peace. But there is that picture, under the paper in front of him.

42 EXT. FT. BENNING - TRAINING - MARSHLANDS - DAY   42

Crandall's helicopter settles onto the sandy ground, and he begins to count...

                    CRANDALL
          One!... Two!...

Five troopers are hopping from his chopper, under the
watchful eyes of Moore and his officers.

                    CRANDALL (cont'd)
          Three!...

He hits the throttles and the Huey lifts off, as the troopers
race smoothly into the jungle-like vegetation. Moore looks
at his officers.

                    MOORE
          Pretty good, huh?

                    METSKER
          Pretty good.

                    MOORE
          There's one problem.

Moore waves in the next Huey, piloted by Too Tall.

INSIDE THE CHOPPER

another squad of men is ready to deploy. As the chopper
settles in, Lt. Herrick rises to lead his men out the door,
but he's met by a stiff arm from Moore, shoving his back into
his seat. Moore shouts over the turbine and blade noise, to
the sergeant next to Herrick--

                    MOORE (cont'd)
          Your officer's dead, what do you do?! He
          just got shot, WHAT DO YOU DO?!

The sergeant--PALMER--is surprised and doesn't react, so
Moore shouts to the man next to him--

                    MOORE (cont'd)
          So he hesitated and he's dead, what do
          you do?! ...Get out of the chopper, get
          out of the chopper!!

They jump to do so--and, their exit scheme disrupted, stumble
over each other and sprawl onto the ground. As the chopper
lifts off it leaves the squad a mess; one man even gets
caught in the landing skid and drops a few feet into a heap.
Moore stands over his troopers and officers.

                    MOORE (cont'd)
          We'll be landing under fire, gentlemen!
          Men will die!

Moore lifts the last man he yelled at--Ernie Savage.

> MOORE (CONT'D)
> Savage, you learn the job of the man above you, and you teach your job to the man below you in rank. THAT GOES FOR EVERY MAN IN THIS OUTFIT! UNDERSTOOD?!!

They get it.

43 INT. MOORE LIVING ROOM - FT. BENNING BASE HOUSING - DAY 43

Julie Moore is hosting a group of Air Cav wives, over a dozen ladies gathered into her small living room, balancing coffee cups and pound cake on their knees. Among them are Barbara Geoghegan from Philadelphia, Catherine Metsker from New Jersey, and ALMA GIVENS, the only black wife there, from Alabama.

> JULIE
> ...And since some of you are new to the Army, and all of us are new to the base, I thought we'd pool our resources and cover whatever questions we have. So let's start with item number one: food. If the commissary is out of something, where's the best place to shop?

> BARBARA
> I tried Big Star and it's okay. But I keep thinking my water's gonna break right in the check out aisle.

> JULIE
> So what you do is, you carry a jar of pickles, and if your water breaks you drop the jar on the floor, it breaks, you're covered.

> BARBARA
> What a great idea!

> JULIE
> I've got five children, you learn all the tricks.

The ladies laugh and begin to chatter, loosening up. We pan their faces: young women, most of them in their early twenties, struggling to keep their families together as their husbands are off at war. And Julie, stepping up to the task of helping them, feels her confidence growing.

JULIE (cont'd)
I guess that takes care of food shopping.
Item number two: laundry.

WIFE
The base washing machines don't work.
They're full of sand from the swamp
missions.

JULIE
I'll see about that.

WIFE
I already complained.

JULIE
Then we'll go to the General if we have
to.

Catherine, youngest of the group, says in a New Jersey accent-

CATHERINE
In the meantime the laundromat in town's
okay, but they won't let you wash colored
things in their machines.

BARBARA
At a public laundromat?

CATHERINE
Doesn't make sense to me, either. But
I'm telling you, they got a big sign
right on the front door, says "Whites
Only."

This brings the meeting to silence. Alma Givens, a formidable black woman, starts to snicker.

CATHERINE (cont'd)
What?

ALMA
Honey, they mean white people only.

The full weight of it hits Catherine.

CATHERINE
I never even thought that such-- That's
awful! Today!...

Alma Givens touches her lips as if to blot off the laughter

                    CATHERINE (cont'd)
          I don't see what's so funny! We'll
          picket that place, they can't get away
          with that! Your husband's wearing the
          uniform of a country that allows a place
          to--to say his laundry's not good enough,
          when he could die for--!

Catherine stops herself; she's uttered the unmentionable.

                    CATHERINE (cont'd)
          I'm sorry, I just--

                    ALMA
          That's all right, Honey. But I know what
          my husband's fighting for, and that's why
          I can smile. He's not fighting laundry.
          He's fighting for his country.

Alma has everybody's attention. Her smile is gone.

                    ALMA (cont'd)
          And in the Army it's better than outside,
          because all that matters here is how
          brave he is, and there's nobody braver!
          I know segregated places are something to
          beat, but everybody fights in his own
          way. My husband will never ask for
          respect, and he'll give respect to no man
          who hasn't earned it. The rest of his
          family is the same way! And anybody who
          doesn't respect that can keep his goddamn
          washing machine--cause my babies' clothes
          are gonna be clean anyway!

When she finishes it's at revival pitch. Then silence.

                    JULIE
          Well. I guess that takes care of item
          number two.

Everybody bursts into laughter and shouts of agreement, the whole room alive and unified, a family of sisters.

Barbara Geoghegan stops laughing and grabs at her belly; she knocks over her coffee cup in a spasm.

                    JULIE (cont'd)
          Okay...okay...we're all calm-- Her
          water's broken! Somebody get a jar of
          pickles!-- A car of pickles!-- A car!!

44   INT. HOSPITAL INFANT STABILIZATION NURSERY - NIGHT   44

   A baby just a few hours fresh from God lies sleeping in a
   newborn bassinet, under a pink card lettered GEOGHEGAN. Hal
   Moore, wearing a clean uniform, pauses outside the sterile
   glass of the nursery, and looks at her.

45   INT. HOSPITAL CHAPEL - NIGHT   45

   Moore enters the chapel, searching, and spots Lt. Geoghegan
   kneeling at a front pew. Seeing the Colonel, Geoghegan,
   wearing a dirty training uniform, jumps to his feet.

                        MOORE
             At ease. I heard one of my new
             lieutenants just became a father. Came
             to say congratulations.

                        GEOGHEGAN
             Thank you, Sir.

   Moore sits; Geoghegan takes a seat on the pew beside him.
   Moore looks up at the candles, and the cross.

                        MOORE
             Didn't mean to disturb you.

                        GEOGHEGAN
             It's all right, Sir.

                        MOORE
             How's your wife?

                        GEOGHEGAN
             Sleeping. So is my daughter. I just
             wanted to pray for awhile, before I held
             her.

   Moore takes a long look at Geoghegan; he's taken an instant
   liking to this young man, who has his heart in his throat.
   Moore's eyes notice the pink baby bracelet on Geoghegan's
   wrist. Geoghegan's embarrassed.

                        GEOGHEGAN (cont'd)
             The nurse gave me this, I just--

                        MOORE
             No, don't take that off.

   Moore sits down beside him.

GEOGHEGAN
Colonel... How do you feel about being a soldier--and a father?

MOORE
I hope being one makes me better at being the other. How about you?

GEOGHEGAN
Between college and here, I spent a year in Africa. We built a school for orphans. They were orphans because the warlord across the border didn't like their tribe. ...I know God has a plan for me. I just hope it's to protect orphans--and not make any.

MOORE
Let's ask him.

Moore kneels on the prayer bench, and crosses himself; Geoghegan, surprised, kneels too.

MOORE (cont'd)
Hail Mary, full of grace...

GEOGHEGAN
Hail Mary, full of grace...

Moore pauses...and departs from the catechism.

MOORE
Our Father in Heaven, before we go into battle, every soldier among us will approach You, each in his own way. Our enemies too, according to their own understanding, will ask for protection, and for victory. And so we bow, before Your infinite wisdom and mystery, and offer our prayers as best we can. I pray You watch over the young men, like Jack Geoghegan, that I lead into battle. Use me as your instrument, in this awful hell of war, to watch over them. And I pray that if anyone must die, that I can give up my life, for theirs. Especially if they are men like this one beside me, deserving of a future in Your blessing and good will. Amen.

GEOGHEGAN
Amen.

> MOORE
> And oh yes, dear Lord, about our
> enemies... Please ignore their heathen
> prayers, and help us blow the little
> bastards straight to hell.

> GEOGHEGAN
> Amen to that too, Sir!

On Hal Moore's eyes, as he looks at this fine young man, young officer, young father, newly under his command, we hear the VOICE OF LYNDON JOHNSON...

> LBJ (V.O)
> It is our duty to defend freedom
> everywhere.

46 QUICK CUTS - ACROSS AMERICA - DAY   46

A montage of America: from Washington, D.C., to small towns, Manhattan streets, farm houses...

> LBJ (V.O.)
> And because of this duty...

We see the ACTUAL NEWS FOOTAGE of President Lyndon Johnson making the announcement:

> LBJ (cont'd)
> ...I have today ordered the 1st Airmobile
> Division to Vietnam.

47 INT. MOORE HOME - DAY   47

Julie and the other wives, assembled for another meeting, have stopped to watch the television, and receive the news in silence. Julie's eyes look numb, and far away.

> JULIE
> Get out your best dress, ladies-- They're
> gonna want to celebrate.

48 EXT. COMMANDING GENERAL'S MANSION - FT. BENNING - NIGHT   48

The officers--about 20 of them--are in their dress uniforms, and their wives are in their prettiest dresses, all gathered under a party tent beneath the oaks of the grounds outside the antebellum residence of the Commanding General. The men are beaming, smoking cigars; Julie is beautiful on Hal's arm, as she and Hal meet General Kinnard.

> MOORE
> And you know my wife--

                    GENERAL KINNARD
          Julie! You look especially lovely
          tonight.

                    JULIE
          Thank you, General. You're so kind to
          open your home to us.

                    GENERAL KINNARD
          I like to see my boys having fun.

At the bandstand, Crandall jumps onstage, consults with the
bandleader, and launches into a song. His buddies and their
ladies dance; Crandall even pulls Too Tall onstage to sing
with him. General Kinnard smiles, but sees Hal lost in
thought.

                    GENERAL KINNARD (cont'd)
          Hal, can I see you a minute?

He leads Hal to a quieter place, under a tree.

                    GENERAL KINNARD (cont'd)
          Why the long face? This deployment's
          quite a tribute to what you've
          accomplished in such a short time.

                    MOORE
          Thank you sir. But I didn't hear the
          President mention a State Of Emergency.

                    GENERAL KINNARD
          No, he didn't.

                    MOORE
          And without that declaration, the
          enlistments will not be extended.

                    GENERAL KINNARD
          I'm sorry, Hal.

                    MOORE
          Forgive me, Sir, but let me get this
          straight. We form a division using
          techniques that have never been attempted
          in battle--against an enemy with twenty
          years of combat experience, on their
          ground, twelve thousand miles from our
          ground. And just before the Army sends
          us into the fight, they take away a third
          of my men. The most experienced third,
          including officers. You saw this coming.
                    (MORE)

                    MOORE (cont'd)
          That's why you sent me that new crop of
          platoon leaders.

     Moore struggles to contain his anger, and face the facts.

                    MOORE (cont'd)
          Korea didn't teach 'em anything.

                    GENERAL KINNARD
          Politicians?

     Crandall leaves the stage, and the band strikes up a tender
     love song. As the other couples slow dance, Julie is left
     alone. Hal sees this and starts toward her, but Kinnard
     stops him one more time.

                    GENERAL KINNARD (cont'd)
          By the way, Hal. Since we're being
          deployed, they're renumbering the units.
          You're now the commander of the 1st
          Battalion of the 7th Cavalry.

                    MOORE
          The 7th? The same regiment as...Custer?

     Kinnard nods soberly. Moore nods and moves toward Julie.
     But she sees something in his eyes as he moves toward her
     from beneath the oaks, their limbs trailing Spanish moss like
     the ghosts of hanged men.

49   INT. MOORE'S HOUSE - KITCHEN - NIGHT   49

     On one corner of the table lies his newly updated "Last Will
     and Testament." Hal's already signed it. Hal sits at the
     table, still in his dress uniform. Two books are open in
     front of him; one is the picture of the slaughter of the
     French Group Mobile unit he studied before; the other is an
     artist's rendering of the stripped and mutilated bodies after
     "Custer's Last Stand."

     Moore's eyes scan from one to the other. The pictures are
     almost identical. In the shadows beyond the doorway stands
     Julie, in her nightgown. She'd like to hold him and be held,
     to make love, but knows the time for that is gone.

50   EXT. GEOGHEGAN'S HOUSE - DAY   50

     The Lieutenant's housing is in a block of plain Ft. Benning
     apartments. Julie knocks on the front door and Barbara opens
     it.

                    BARBARA
          Julie! Come in!

                    JULIE
          I brought some Rit dye. You have to make
          all the underwear jungle green, and I
          figured you might not have time to get by
          the Piggly Wiggly.

51   As Julie enters she spots Jack Geoghegan, sitting by the   51
     window with his new baby daughter in his arms.

                    BARBARA
          Julie, my husband, Jack--

                    JULIE
          Nice to meet you, Jack, please, keep your
          seat.

But he's already jumping to his feet, cradling the baby.

                    JACK
          Nice to meet you! The Colonel gave us
          time off to spend with our families.

Julie smiles softly...and a bit sadly.

52   CLOSE - A BOILING POT   52

with several packets of dye thrown in. Barbara stirs the big
pot, dipping up an undershirt to check its color; but her
thoughts aren't on the underwear.

                    BARBARA
          You're so prepared.

                    JULIE
          My father was an Artillery Officer. It's
          just second nature to me now.

                    BARBARA
          I should've been ready.

                    JULIE
          Nobody's ready for her husband to go to
          war. We just do what we have to, like
          they do.

Barbara looks through the doorway into the living room, where
Jack sits nuzzling the baby. She lowers her voice.

                    BARBARA
          I just don't know if I can. I mean, I
          will, it's just... I love Jack so much,
          but he's supposed to be here, with me and
          Cammie.

Barbara wipes tears from her eyes and holds back more; but Julie's gentle silence encourages her to open up.

                    BARBARA (cont'd)
          We worked for the church, he could've had
          a deferment! But now...

                    JULIE
          You're mad at him.

                    BARBARA
          No. Yes.

Julie fishes a forkful of underwear into a strainer.

                    JULIE
          I'm the daughter of a soldier, and the
          wife of one. But I can't explain 'em.
          Today when Hal told the other officers to
          go home to their families, he stayed at
          his desk, to work. He's the toughest man
          I've ever known, and the softest, and
          I've never seen him cry.

CLOSE ON JULIE MOORE. Her eyes tell the story of every woman who has ever watched a husband go off to war.

                    JULIE (cont'd)
          I don't know what to tell you...Except
          this. Do you know the most common thing
          that American soldiers say when they know
          they're dying on the battlefield?

Barbara doesn't know.

                    JULIE (cont'd)
          "Tell my wife I love her."

Barbara walks slowly from the kitchen, moves to Jack, and wraps her arms around both him and her daughter.

Julie watches from the doorway, wishing she could hold her husband in the same way.

53   EXT. THE AIR CAVALRY CELEBRATION - DAY   53

The Air Cav patch, emblazoned with a horse head, is stenciled along with crossed cavalry sabres onto the noses of helicopters racing in formation across Ft. Benning and past the parade ground bleachers full of people.

The Army Band is playing "Garry Owen," a stirring Irish drinking tune that is the theme of the 7th Cavalry.

The American flag and brigade colors with battle streamers curl in the breeze, carried by an honor guard in black stetsons, blue shirts, and tan britches above riding boots.

The 1st battalion of the 7th Air Cav marches in with them, Hal Moore and his staff in the lead, all of them wearing the black stetson.

The wives and families are gathered in the bleachers, along with the dignitaries on the platform, and they are stirred by the spectacle, the drums, the emotion of the moment.

A bugler plays the Cavalry's CHARGE, and Crandall's squadron of Hueys roar in and settle to earth at one end of the field, as a V formation of Phantom jets scream overhead.

A cheer goes up from the men, and then a CHANT...

                    TROOPERS
        Air-Cav!   Air-Cav!   Air-Cav!

IN THE BLEACHERS, the wives too are caught up in the infectious enthusiasm; feeling the pulse of the military snare and the punctuated shouts of the men, the black wives begin to dance, and the white wives join them, laughing.

A RIDER on a black stallion, outfitted exactly like a trooper from Ft. Apache, appears at one end of the parade ground; the drummers thunder into sudden SILENCE. The rider moves along the length of parade ground between the bleachers and the troopers, and comes to a halt at Crandall's chopper.

Another cheer goes up from the crowd and the men. OUT AMONG THE FORMATION OF TROOPERS are Adams, Beck, and Ouellette.

                    OUELLETTE
        I don't get it--we gonna take horses on
        the choppers?

                    BECK
        No, you idiot, it's a symbol. The old
        becomes the new--or the new is the old--
        some shit, hell, I don't know.

                    ADAMS
        Great. The 7th Cavalry.

                    OUELLETTE
        What's wrong with the 7th Cavalry?

                    BECK
        The 7th Cavalry was Custer's.

                    OUELLETTE
          ...Yeah?...

                    ADAMS
          Custer? The battle of the Little Big
          Horn?

                    OUELLETTE
          Who won there?

                    BECK
          The Indians. Massacred the entire 7th
          Cavalry.

                    OUELLETTE
          ...Cool!

UP ON THE DAIS, crowded with dignitaries, General Kinnard is
finishing his remarks.

                    GENERAL KINNARD
          ...And we know you will honor your
          country, your families, and yourselves in
          your service to all.

He receives polite applause from the families and brass.

                    GENERAL KINNARD (cont'd)
          Our final remarks will be from Lt.
          Colonel Moore, field commander of the 7th
          Cavalry.

The applause is spirited as Moore steps to the microphone.
He looks out over his men, at their families...and at Julie.

                    MOORE
          Look around you. In the 7th Cavalry
          we've got a Captain born in the Ukraine,
          another from Puerto Rico, a platoon
          leader from Wales. We've got Japanese,
          Chinese, Blacks, Hispanics, Cherokee
          Indians, Jews and Gentiles--all
          Americans.

As he says this we pick out some individual faces, like
Savage, Adams, Beck, Geoghegan...

                    MOORE (cont'd)
          Here, in the States, some men in this
          unit will experience discrimination
          because of race, or creed. But for you
          and me, all that is gone.
                         (MORE)

                    MOORE (CONT'D)
          Where we're going, you'll watch the back
          of the man next to you, as he will watch
          yours, and you won't care what color he
          is, or by what name he calls God. They
          say we're leaving home. But we are going
          to what home was always supposed to be.

Everyone applauds; the dignitaries love this; the couple of
REPORTERS in attendance are scribbling.

                    MOORE (cont'd)
          So let us understand the situation. We
          are going into battle, against a tough
          and determined enemy. I can't promise
          you that I will bring you all home alive.

The mood changes among the dignitaries; nobody talks of death
in send-off speeches. The Chaplain's Bible is lying on the
podium; Moore places his hand over it.

                    MOORE (CONT'D)
          But I swear this, before you and before
          Almighty God. When we go into battle, I
          will be the first to step onto the field,
          and I will be the last to step off. And
          I will leave no one behind. Dead or
          alive. We will all come home. Together.

Absolute silence. He steps away from the microphone. His
eyes find Julie. Everyone there--especially Julie Moore--
knows he meant every word.

Only the hot moist wind stirs across the parade ground.

54   INT. MOORE'S APARTMENT - NIGHT   54

The family has dinner. Hal, Julie, and all five kids; it's
quiet, nobody has much to say. The older boys are excited,
especially Greg.

                    GREG
          Wow, Dad. All the choppers, huh?
          Everybody moving out together!

                    MOORE
          Everybody, yeah.

                    GREG
          Wow, that's so great!

                    MOORE
          Okay, everybody ready for bed.

                    CECILE
          Daddy, will you read to me?

                    MOORE
          Sure, Honey.

55   INT. MOORE'S APARTMENT - MASTER BEDROOM - NIGHT   55

     Hal sits on the bed with his young daughter Cecile. He pulls
     her onto his lap and starts going through the books she's
     brought him.

                    MOORE
          Okay, let's see... Winnie the Pooh,
          these, what is it, Bears? Or...

                    CECILE
          Daddy, what is a war?

                    MOORE
          War?

     In the bathroom, Julie freezes over the sink.

                    MOORE (cont'd)
          It...It's something that shouldn't
          ...but, it does...happen. It... it's
          when some people in one country try to
          take away...the lives of other people,
          and...well, then soldiers like your Daddy
          have to go over and stop them.

                    CECILE
          Are they gonna try to take your life
          away, Daddy?

     Silence; Julie pops in.

                    JULIE
          Come on, Cecile, time for bed.

                    MOORE
          Yes, Cecile, they're gonna try. And I'm
          not gonna let 'em.

                    CECILE
          Okay, Daddy!

     She kisses him, and goes off to bed peacefully.

56   INT. BEDROOM - NIGHT   56

     Hal and Julie lie side by side in the darkness.

                    HAL
          I have to be up at 1:30, to be at the
          buses before the men start getting there.
          I'll let you sleep.

     She wants to say something; she doesn't know how. They just
     hold each other, in the dark silence of the night.

57   INT. MOORE'S BEDROOM - THE CLOCK, READING 1:30   57

     Hal rises. Julie's back is to him as he dresses, and he
     can't see her face; she is awake, and fighting with every bit
     of her strength not to let herself cry, to make his leaving
     harder for him, for her, for their children.

     Thinking she is still asleep, he leans and touches his lips
     to the surface of her hair; she knows he's there, and tears
     slide silently across her face and down upon her pillow.

     She hears the door close softly, and now she can't stop the
     tears from flowing.

58   EXT. MOORE'S HOUSE - NIGHT   58

     Moore steps from his family's home, into the deserted street.
     He forces himself not to stop, he tries not to think of the
     family he is leaving, perhaps forever. He slings his
     soldier's pack of personal belongings onto his shoulders, and
     walks down the street, into the night.

     The door of the Moore house opens suddenly and Julie rushes
     out, in her robe. He has gone.

                    JULIE
          I love you...

59   EXT. FT. BENNING PARADE GROUND - NIGHT   59

     Buses are waiting; Moore is the first to arrive. Then Jack
     Geoghegan shows up, followed by a grinning Henry Herrick, who
     seems enthusiastic about going to war.

     FROM THE BARRACKS ACROSS THE STREET, the enlisted men come
     double-timing, carrying their gear, their boots hitting the
     pavement like distant thunder.

     THE BUS TIRES begin to roll, as the air brakes hiss off. Hal
     Moore is in the front seat of the first bus, his face
     gleaming green from the dash lights, his features set toward
     war.

As the bus passes we seen the face of Jack Geoghegan, and he looks like a boy going off to school, glancing back toward home, and his family.

60 EXT. CAMP HOLLOWAY - DAY   60

Establishing an encampment in the badlands of Vietnam. It's an Army city, sprung up like a frontier boomtown. Moore and Plumley stride quickly through the camp and enter

61 INT. COMMAND HUT - DAY   61

Moore and Plumley move into the command hut--a wooden structure complete with a window air conditioning unit--where COLONEL BROWN and an INTELLIGENCE OFFICER are standing over a map.

> COLONEL BROWN
> Last night the enemy hit our camp at Plei Me.

> MOORE
> How many casualties?

> COLONEL BROWN
> None. The enemy force withdrew toward this mountain near the Cambodian border. How many men do you have battle-ready, give or take?

> MOORE
> Sergeant Major?

> PLUMLEY
> Three hundred ninety-five. Exactly.

> MOORE
> What do you estimate the enemy strength?

> INTELLIGENCE OFFICER
> We appraise their numbers as manageable.

> MOORE
> You have no idea.

> COLONEL BROWN
> We have no idea.

Moore fingers the map, where a red star marks Chu Pong Mountain, above the Ia Drang Valley.

                              COLONEL BROWN (CONT'D)
                         Simple orders, Hal. Find the enemy. And
                         kill him.

62   EXT. CAMP HOLLOWAY - DAY   62

        Moore and Plumley walk out of the command hut. Moore stops,
        his mind tumbling.

                              MOORE
                         They attack with no casualties, then run
                         for the mountains, so we'll chase 'em.
                         That smell like an ambush to you?

                              PLUMLEY
                         They get close enough to kill us, they'll
                         be close enough to kill.

                              MOORE
                         It's a half hour round trip by chopper.
                         So the first sixty men to go in will be
                         all alone for thirty minutes. Think you
                         ought to get an M-16?

                              PLUMLEY
                         Time comes I need one, Sir, they'll be
                         plenty of 'em lyin' on the ground.

63   THE AIR CAV ASSAULT - VARIOUS SHOTS - DAY   63

        Sixteen Huey helicopters are lined up in formation; Moore's
        troopers are formed up in their battle gear, He looks them
        over, and without a word he crosses the red clay ground and
        steps into Crandall's helicopter, accompanied by Plumley,
        Metsker, Air Controller CHARLIE HASTINGS, radio operator
        Ouellette, and MR. NIK, their translator.

        EXT. CAMP/INTERIOR CHOPPERS - DAY

        Air Cav troopers stream to Too Tall's chopper and to the
        other helicopters, tucking in, preparing for battle.
        Physically they are ready, but now the awful, internal part
        comes. Their mouths are dry from the terror that surges
        through every soldier before battle. Some tremble from the
        adrenaline. Some pray. All are wide-eyed and stressed. But
        every man knows his job, and every man is ready to go.

        One trooper, holding a puppy he's adopted, hands it to a huge
        black enlisted man who's staying behind.

64 INT. CRANDALL'S CHOPPER - DAY   64

CRANDALL fires up a big cigar, and shoves the throttles; his chopper lifts into the air; the others follow.

The rest of Moore's men are scattered in companies at pick up zones, awaiting their turn to fly into their first major combat. As the helicopters lift off and stream overhead, it is almost worse for the men left behind, to sit and wait...

> VOICE OVER
> It was Nov 14, 1965. A Sunday. The assault on Landing Zone X-Ray had begun.

65 EXT. BASE CHURCH - DAY   65

> CHAPLAIN'S VOICE
> And for our offertory hymn, Catherine Metsker.

66 INT. BASE CHURCH - DAY   66

The families left behind have gathered to worship and pray for their men. The wives with their children are near the front pews; the church is full. The base CHAPLAIN steps away from the pulpit.

Catherine, a bit pale, moves from the choir to the front of the church as the pianist plays the first few notes of an old hymn, "The Solid Rock." Catherine sings, shakily...

> CATHERINE
> "My hope is built on nothing less
> Than Jesus' blood and righteousness
> I dare not trust the sweetest..."

The emotion chokes her voice; she stops. The pianist stops. Catherine whispers...

> CATHERINE (cont'd)
> Sorry...

She nods for the pianist to begin again.

> CATHERINE (cont'd)
> "My hope is built on nothing less
> Than Jesus' blood..."

She stops again, emotion errupting below the surface. In that horrible silence Julie begins singing the familiar chorus...

                    JULIE
          "On Christ the solid rock I stand..."

                    JULIE AND BARBARA
          "All other ground is sinking sand..."

                    ALL WIVES JOINING IN
          "All other ground is sinking sand."

Drawing strength from her friends, Catherine leads them on
the next verse, her voice growing stronger with every word.

                    CATHERINE
          "When he shall come with trumpet sound,
          O may I then in him be found.
          Clothed in his righteousness alone,
          Faultless to stand before the throne.
          On Christ the solid rock I stand,
          All other ground is sinking sand,
          All other ground is sinking sand."

67   A GECKO, ULTRA CLOSE, clings to a tree; his tongue flicks the   67
     air, tasting danger. He scurries to earth, just as a shell
     screams out of the sky and explodes onto

68   LZ X-RAY - DAY   68

     The artillery barrage begins, meant to soften up any
     resistance around the clearing.

     SUPERIMPOSE:

                         10:17 A.M.

69   HIGH ON CHU PONG MASSIF - DAY   69

     In a bunker tucked on the side of the mountain, moving into
     the lantern light above a table of maps is the fearsome,
     scarred face of Colonel Ahn. He hears the artillery,
     crashing down into the valley below. An OFFICER on his staff
     hurries in.

                    NVA OFFICER
                (subtitled Vietnamese)
          The helicopter soldiers are coming.

     Exactly as Ahn expected.

                    AHN
          Get them ready.

     His officer runs out, to--

70   OUTSIDE AHN'S BUNKER, in an encampment brilliantly camouflaged from the air, is a whole army of North Vietnamese, preparing for battle. We see the People's Army of Vietnam troopers--hundreds...thousands of them. The NVA Officer starts shouting orders.

71   MONTAGE - THE AIR CAV FLIES OFF TO BATTLE

We see the choppers in the air, in formation...

The individual soldiers... Hal Moore... Plumley... Metsker... Hastings... and Ouellette... Crandall at the controls, with MILLS, his copilot... and Moore again.

In the other choppers, friends look at each other, or try to look at nothing at all.

At first the chopper formation is high, to avoid ground fire. Crandall speaks to Moore as well as the other chopper pilots, through the headset.

> CRANDALL
> Two miles out. Dropping to nap of the earth...

Crandall noses down, and they race above the trees, toward death and glory. Birds scatter beneath them; the skids of the choppers brush the treetops.

72   EXT. LANDING ZONE X-RAY - DAY

Preparatory artillery and rocket fire are lighting up the landing zone; it suddenly ceases.

THE SUN is a huge red ball at the horizon...and racing in from it, with a DEAFENING ROAR, are

EIGHT ASSAULT HELICOPTERS

They flare to cut speed and settle onto the grass.

SUPERIMPOSE:

> 10:48 A.M.

As Crandall's chopper settles to earth, Moore unhooks his seat belt, switches the selector switch of his M-16 to full auto, and jumps out, his boots the first on the ground. He lands running, leading Plumley and the men from the first wave of choppers across the grass where the recent artillery still smolders.

They fire covering bursts from their weapons, charging the treeline, as behind them the first wave of choppers roars off and the second settles in, men jumping out before the skids touch, fifty in all, following Moore.

They reach the trees unopposed, plunge across a waist deep, ten-foot wide dry creekbed, and into the scrub brush. As the helicopters lift off behind them, the clearing is left in complete SILENCE.

The silence is unearthly. It is wrong.

Moore takes it in, his senses straining at the silence, sniffing the danger. He signals TONY NADAL, a 29 year-old Captain from Puerto Rico, who sends two patrols to fan out; one moves off cautiously, but the other, led by the enthusiastic Lt. Herrick, moves far too quickly up and beyond the creekbed. Uneasily hurrying behind their green lieutenant are Squad Leader Sergeant Ernie Savage, Platoon Sergeant Palmer and a trooper named BUNGUM.

> PALMER
> Bungum, I'll be forty years old day after tomorrow, but I don't believe I will live to see it.

> BUNGUM
> Come on, Sarge, you can't be out here with that kind of attitude. You'll make it.

MOORE gives the hand signal for his command group to circle up on him, and he takes in the terrain: a grassy clearing no larger than a football field, surrounded by brush and trees, beside a sprawling Vietnamese mountain.

> OUELLETTE
> Hey! I got something! It's a boy!

Plumley moves up to see what Ouellette is pointing his rifle at.

> PLUMLEY
> Hell, that ain't no boy.

He grabs a trembling North Vietnamese soldier, pulls him up out of the grass. Mr. Nik begins spouting Vietnamese.

MOORE is giving orders to Metsker.

> MOORE
> Keep the patrols in tight contact.

                    PLUMLEY
          Colonel, we got a prisoner.

Moore moves to the trembling Vietnamese soldier.

                    MR. NIK
          He say he deserter.

                    PLUMLEY
          Bullshit, he's a lookout.

                    MOORE
          Ask him if there's any North Vietnamese
          around here.

Mr. Nik rattles off the Vietnamese; the prisoner answers, and Mr. Nik pauses, pale.

                    MR. NIK
          He say this area is base camp of whole
          division. Ten thousand men.

The prisoner has suddenly become talkative; Nik translates--

                    MR. NIK (cont'd)
          Same army that destroyed French at Dien
          Ben Phu. He say they want very badly
          kill Americans. Just not been able to
          find any yet.

Moore and his men look toward the mountain beside them.

                    MOORE
          Call the patrols back. We've got to
          regroup and engage the enemy as far from
          the landing zone as--

THE RATTLE OF GUNFIRE breaks the stillness; at first it comes from up the creekbed, where Herrick's patrol has gone; then suddenly the air around Moore is alive with bullets.

                    MOORE (CONT'D)
          Come on, we've got to attack!

Ouellette starts to run toward the creekbed and the gunfire; Moore grabs him, and points toward the edge of the mountain, behind them.

                    MOORE (CONT'D)
          They'll come that way!

He leads his men, running toward the mountain trails.

THE AMERICANS' POV plunges the audience into the abrupt chaos; wild, swinging visual pandemonium, intensified by a stunning turmoil of sound--gunfire, shouts, explosions, and the thundering detonations of redlining heartbeats.

They fall to the earth and begin returning fire at the North Vietnamese Army (NVA), attacking from the trees and grass. Moore shouts to Metsker, who is beside him on the radio.

                    MOORE (cont'd)
          What's happening with that patrol?

                    METSKER
          Trying to reach them, Sir!

73 EXT. HERRICK'S PLATOON - DAY   73

Lt. Herrick, a former football player, is eagerly chasing a few NVA soldiers fleeing into the brush.

                    HERRICK
          There they are! Come on!

He fires another burst and takes off in pursuit. Savage thinks it's a bad idea--

                    SAVAGE
          But sir--

Herrick is racing off, and Savage and the other twenty-seven men in the patrol hurry to follow...but the air is cut by the supersonic crack of bullets flying past.

Herrick seems not to notice, until a hole opens in the helmet of his radio operator, and the man falls dead beside him. Herrick stops, as his mind tries to comprehend... He orders another trooper--

                    HERRICK
          You--take the radio--

The man steps forward, and is shot too.

The first blood of battle. The young Americans freeze in shock; then Savage reacts first, firing at the enemy moving out of the trees; he sprays down five men in a few seconds, and other troopers begin to fire grenades from their M-79 launchers, and bursts from their M-16 rifles. Herrick is still intent on chasing the NVA.

                    HERRICK (cont'd)
          Come on, they're getting away!

                          PALMER
                Sir, look!

He points out the NVA moving through the trees around them.
And another American goes down.

                          HERRICK
                Fall back!

The Americans start to move back in the direction they came,
dragging their dead and wounded with them. Savage is
bringing up the rear, covering the retreat, firing first
left, then right, then to the front; they are under attack
from three sides now.

And then they see it--the NVA has closed off the fourth side
too. The American patrol is completely cut off, on a knoll
with no cover, just the elephant grass.

                          HERRICK (cont'd)
                Come on, I'll get us out of--

A bullet shatters his hip. The medic, CHARLIE LOSE, moves to
him. Everyone is crouching, frozen.

                          PALMER
                Grab the wounded! We'll make a run for
                that--

A bullet drops Palmer too; he falls beside Bungum.

                          BUNGUM
                Sarge...? SARGE!!??

Another Sergeant stands up.

                          SERGEANT
                We've got to get out of here!

A bullet slaps into his spine, and he falls dead.

The survivors dive to the earth in absolute terror. For a
moment, Ernie Savage is as scared as everybody. Then--

                          SAVAGE
                Don't anybody move! Stay down!

74   EXT. THE LANDING ZONE - MOORE'S GROUP - DAY   74

Moore's group of men are screaming--into radios, at the
enemy, at each other. His shout cuts above theirs.

                    MOORE
          HEY!

They turn, wild-eyed, to look at him. He says, with icy
calm, as quietly as possible above the noise--

                    MOORE (cont'd)
          Calm down. Understand the situation, and
          communicate clearly.

He speaks as if they're inside a classroom--then turns calmly
and sprays an M-16 burst into two North Vietnamese racing at
them, not twenty feet away, and cuts them down.

                    MOORE (cont'd)
          Pull the chain on all the firepower you
          can put onto that mountain.

As Metsker relays the order, Plumley taps Moore's arm to
point out two more North Vietnamese running in from the
opposite direction, and Moore sprays them down too. The
evidence that they are totally surrounded threatens to panic
everyone again, but Moore remains calm.

                    MOORE (cont'd)
          Alert Crandall that the landing zone is
          under fire.

Ouellette starts talking into the field radios.

75   INT. HELICOPTER - BRUCE CRANDALL - DAY   75

Crandall, piloting his chopper as bullets ping around his
cockpit, hears--

                    RADIO VOICE
          ...under fire, repeat, under fire.

                    CRANDALL
          No shit.

With Too Tall's chopper just off his side, Crandall flies
straight at the landing zone, through the hail of gunfire,
bringing in the second wave of troopers, who feel sure they
will die before they reach the ground.

76   INT. NORTH VIETNAMESE BUNKER - COLONEL AHN - DAY   76

An NVA OFFICER turns from his field phone and tells Ahn--

                    NVA OFFICER
          They've put up stiff resistance precisely
          where we are attacking!

                    AHN
          Shift immediately to their flanks. Do
          not let them breathe.

77   EXT. LZ X-RAY - MOORE AND PLUMLEY - DAY   77

     Plumley has taken a position back to back with Moore, like
     buddies in a bar fight. Metsker turns grimly from his radio.

                    METSKER
          Herrick's platoon is cut off and under
          attack. B Company is holding.

                    MOORE
          They're gonna try to flank us.

     Bullets are cutting across the landing zone and into the
     choppers; the second lift is landing under heavy fire. Moore
     runs out and shouts to the reinforcements in Crandall's
     chopper--

                    MOORE (cont'd)
          Get into the trees over there and prepare
          to be attacked in force! MOVE!!

     THE NEW ARRIVALS

     race toward the position Moore indicated; several drop from
     the enemy fire singing across the landing zone. They reach
     the tree line and fall to the ground. There is no time to
     dig holes; they lie flat and place spare ammo clips in front
     of them.

     MOORE waves the choppers away--and sees Mr. Nik jump into the
     last chopper, fleeing. Ouellette, ducking gunfire, catches
     up to Moore, who grabs the radio handset.

                    MOORE (cont'd)
               (into radio)
          We are taking casualties. Order Doc
          Carrara and his medical aid station to
          come in. Don't bother with the tent--but
          bring a lot of supplies.

78   AT THE CUT-OFF PLATOON   78

     Bullets zing around Charlie Lose, the only Medic among the
     seventeen men cut off on the isolated mound, who is kneeling
     above Herrick and shoving compresses into his huge wounds.

                    HERRICK
          Savage...don't let 'em get the signals
          codes. ...I'm glad I could die for my
          country.

He dies. Medic Lose closes his Lieutenant's eyes.

Bungum is crying, lying next to Palmer; then he hears--

                    PALMER
          Bungum...

                    BUNGUM
              (brightening)
          Sarge!

                    PALMER
          ...Tell my wife I love her.

Bungum, to his horror, sees Palmer die too.

Ernie Savage sees the panic rising all around him. It's up to him. He grabs the radio and spreads out his grid map.

                    SAVAGE
              (into radio)
          This is Savage. We'll need artillery, to
          these coordinates...

79   EXT. AMERICAN ARTILLERY, LZ FALCON - DAY   79

The howitzers are set up in a line, in a position carved out of the jungle.

SUPERIMPOSE:

              Landing Zone Falcon
              Five Miles From X-Ray

The gunners begin to fire in salvo, cascades of flame leaping from the throats of the howitzers.

80   OUT BY THE CREEK BED, AND THE CUT-OFF PLATOON   80

The NVA, highly disciplined and fearless, work their way forward, closing in for the kill...when suddenly a wall of artillery rips into the ground between them and the cut-off platoon.

81   INT. NVA BUNKER - ON THE MOUNTAIN - DAY   81

Colonel Ahn stands in a lantern-lit yet intensely well-coordinated command center, where his men constantly upgrade his map information. An NVA MAJOR relays a field phone report--

                    NVA MAJOR
          They are using artillery as a shield! It
          is accurate, and continuous.

                    AHN
          We must overrun them now, when they are
          at their weakest!
              (jabbing map)
          Attack here, here, and here! Overwhelm
          the landing zone, and we have choked
          their route of supply and escape!

The officers run out, shouting orders to the troops, massed and waiting for battle. The NVA troops seem endless.

82   ON THE MOUNTAINSIDE   82

500 North Vietnamese, an entire battalion, are already moving down the trails toward the cut-off platoon.

83   EXT. LZ X-RAY - DAY   83

Moore runs in the open, waving the next flight of helicopters to the safest spot. The bullets whizzing by Moore's head sound like a swarm of bees; the ground fire from automatic weapons is so intense that the helicopters don't land, they just hover a few feet above the ground while the troopers jump off, with Moore yelling to their Captain, Bob Edwards--

                    MOORE
          They're trying to run right through us!
          Reinforce Alpha Company, there!

Edwards and his men take off toward the base of the mountain. Moore runs to another chopper, for the medical staff--DOC CARRARA, plus two others.

                    MOORE (cont'd)
          The wounded are behind that mound!

As the doctor and his medical helpers run toward the wounded, Moore turns to run after Edwards, but feels a big hand clap him on the shoulder.

                    PLUMLEY
          Sir, if you don't find some cover you're
          going to go down, and if you go down we
          all go down.

     As the helicopters lift away, shooting their way out with
     their door guns blazing, Moore and Plumley race across the
     open ground toward a termite hill at the edge of the LZ.

     EDWARDS AND HIS MEN sprint to the tree line, dropping from
     their run, and firing.

84   EXT. LZ X-RAY - BEHIND A TERMITE HILL - DAY   84

     Moore and Plumley run through the gunfire. Termite hills--
     hard mounds eight feet high and ten feet wide at the base--
     are a feature of the landscape; Moore and Plumley reach one
     of them, where the six other men of his command unit have
     taken cover; but since they are under attack from several
     directions, bullets sing around them, striking the mound
     beside them, kicking up puffs of dust at their feet, zinging
     by their heads. Ouellette, Moore's radio operator, hands him
     the handset.

                    MOORE
               (into radio)
          Trojan 6.

                    EDWARDS (ON RADIO)
          Colonel, these guys are regulars--

85   INTERCUT - The speaker is Captain Bob Edwards, with the thin 85
     line of new arrivals. They haven't had time to scratch holes
     in the ground; they are under heavy attack.

                    EDWARDS (cont'd)
          --heavily armed, AK-47's and pouches of
          grenades, with heavy machine guns and
          shoulder-fired rockets!

     A human wave of NVA slam into Edwards' position, and the
     fighting is ferocious. The noise and confusion are stunning
     all around Edwards, who must turn and fight for his life--

86   AT THE TERMITE MOUND   86

     Moore hears the pandemonium through the radio: the firing
     and the shouting...

                    RADIO SCREAMS
          --Medic! I'm hit!
          --Mama! I'm dying...
          --Motherfuckers!

87 INT. NVA BUNKER - ON THE MOUNTAIN - DAY   87

Colonel Ahn is on his own radio, talking to the Major.

>   AHN
> Have we broken through?

88 INTERCUT - THE NVA MAJOR, ON A COM-WIRE FIELD RADIO   88

>   NVA MAJOR
> The Americans landed another wave of reinforcements, and they massed precisely where we attacked.
>
>   AHN
> Use the creek bed.

89 Ahn lowers the radio; he has a calm intensity like Moore's. 89

>   AHN (cont'd)
> Their leader is very good. I hope our snipers kill him.

90 EXT. TERMITE MOUND - DAY   90

Bullets are zinging over his head; Moore ignores them, his eyes sweeping from Edwards' position to the right flank.

>   MOORE
>   (into radio)
> Captain Nadal!

91 EXT. THE AMERICAN LINES, NEAR THE CREEKBED - DAY   91

Nadal and his troops crouch in the elephant grass.

>   NADAL
>   (into radio)
> Yes, Colonel?!

92 INTERCUT MOORE, under fire at the termite mound.   92

>   MOORE
>   (into radio)
> Captain Nadal, that creek bed is vital! They'll be coming at you! Do not let them flank! Repeat, do not let them flank!

93   NADAL   93
> Get gunners on our left! Now!

Adams and Beck are with Nadal, who slaps their backs.

                         NADAL (cont'd)
                    Move!

     They race off.

94   FOLLOW ADAMS AND BECK   94

          as they run forward, Adams holding an M-60 machine gun (a
          big, belt-fed beast of a weapon) firing it from the hip, as
          Beck assists, carrying ammo and the shooting stand. To their
          right is a second gun team.

          NVA are visible through the trees, running parallel, racing
          to flank them, while firing. Another ammo bearer, near Beck,
          gets hit with machine gun fire and drops screaming--

          Beck dives for cover, beside an American soldier on the
          ground in a firing position; the guy is looking at Beck.
          Beck looks more closely and sees that the man beside him has
          a small hole in his forehead; he's dead.

                              ADAMS
                    Ammo!

          Beck runs to him and they reload the M-60 with a fresh belt
          of ammo, then stand there together, firing at the attacking
          waves of enemy...

95   EXT. EDGE OF LZ X-RAY - MOORE'S COMMAND POST - DAY   95

          Moore sees his medics overwhelmed already. There are twelve
          wounded men bleeding onto their ponchos in the grassy area
          behind the termite mound--and six dead, lying beneath their
          ponchos a few feet away. And the battlefield medics are
          dragging more killed and wounded troopers in all the time.
          Moore turns to Metsker.

                              MOORE
                    Tom, raise Medevac. We've got to get our
                    wounded out--

          But Metsker interrupts by raising his M-16 and firing; a
          squad of NVA have penetrated the clearing and are racing at
          them. Moore and Plumley fire at them too...

          Metsker is shot, and drops. Moore and Plumley finish off the
          charging NVA, and turn to Metsker. He's hit badly, in the
          shoulder. Plumley presses a field bandage to Metsker's
          wound.

                              PLUMLEY
                    Medic!

Moore's face is stiff; things are getting desperate. He grabs the radio.

96 IN THE HELICOPTERS   96

Crandall and his copilot Mills are leading the helicopters back to the base when they hear the radio traffic.

> MOORE (ON RADIO)
> Medevac, this is 7th Cav. Imperative, repeat imperative, that our wounded be evacuated.

> MEDEVAC PILOT (ON RADIO)
> 7th Cav, this is Medevac, and that is a negative. We cannot fly into a hot landing zone. Please advise when landing zone secure.

Crandall shouts to Mills.

> CRANDALL
> They'll go anyplace except where you need 'em!

97 EXT. LZ X-RAY - MOORE'S COMMAND POST - DAY   97

Moore curses Medevac beneath his breath, and takes in the desperate situation around him. Bullets from the surrounding fight are singing around them. Metsker lies bleeding among a growing mass of wounded men, while Carrara and his two medics and even some of Moore's officers are trying to save them.

> MOORE
> Listen to me! This enemy wants to kill us all, and with numbers in his favor he'll swarm us, that's how he thinks! We've gotta put more artillery onto that mountain! Hastings, get the air support in here! NOW!

Charlie Hastings, the Air Controller, works beside Moore, furiously calling in coordinates...and

98 AERIAL ROCKET ARTILLERY HELICOPTERS wheel in, with a whoosh delivering rockets, with shattering blasts, into the NVA troops running down the mountain trails.   98

FIGHTER-BOMBERS roar across the sky dropping 250 and 500 pound bombs and fearsome napalm canisters.

AT THE TERMITE MOUND, it is a scene from hell. Doc Carrara and the two medics are overwhelmed.

Five feet from Moore, a young trooper, the one who had the puppy, is bleeding to death, convulsing, reaching out... and Moore must ignore him, to keep doing what he must do to keep everyone--anyone--alive.

While on another part of the battlefield...

99 EXT. THE CUT-OFF PLATOON - DAY   99

Savage and the others are hunkered down; an enemy grenade falls to earth and explodes in front of a trooper who jumps up, screaming. Shrapnel is smoking and burning in his face.

                    SAVAGE
          It's phosphorous!

Savage and Bungum trip the trooper and use their bayonets to scrape and dig the burning white phosphorous out of his face. The enemy is suddenly rising out of the grass, attacking them from three directions. Savage grabs two wounded men.

                    SAVAGE (cont'd)
          Come on!

He pulls them to the north side of the knoll, where their line is weakest. Savage fires a grenade launcher knocking down two NVA almost on top of them.

The wounded men fight, and we see their individual acts of courage; one takes a round through his right hand, shifts his rifle to his left hand, and continues firing until he is hit a second time; another is struck by a bullet above his heart that exits under his left arm; bleeding heavily, he grabs a rifle and fights on.

Charlie "Doc" Lose, the medic, crawls from man to man, bandaging them under fire. He has no compresses left, so he rips off his T-shirt and uses that on one man.

The North Vietnamese attack ends as unexpectedly as it began. The Americans on the knoll are shot up, bloody.

                    DOC LOSE
          Anybody have any more bandages?
              (nobody)
          Give me your toilet paper.

They toss him toilet paper packets from their packs, and he uses that to make compresses.

                    SAVAGE
          Redistribute the ammo. Everybody get a
          weapon that works.

                    BUNGUM
          Will our guys come for us, Ernie?

                    SAVAGE
          Sure they will.

He tries to believe it.

100   EXT. THE TERMITE MOUND - DAY   100

      Moore sees his officers working efficiently, and grabs the
      handset from a radio operator--

                    MOORE
          I want that platoon rescued.

101   EXT. IN THE CREEK BED - DAY   101

      Captain Nadal is just climbing into the creekbed with a
      wounded man on his back. He lays him down and grabs the
      radio. All around him his medics are attending wounded. One
      black medic gives a white soldier mouth to mouth.

                    RADIO OPERATOR
          Captain Nadal!

      Nadal takes the handset. Nadal talks while moving along the
      creekbed, pulling troopers back to safety.

                    NADAL
          We just tried another assault, Colonel!
          Lt. Marm took out a machine gun by
          himself, and we still couldn't break
          through!

102   EXT. MOORE'S COMMAND POST - DAY   102

      Moore hears a radio report, and tells Plumley--

                    MOORE
          They couldn't get through to the cut-off
          platoon. And our north and east sides
          are wide open.

103   INT. CRANDALL'S HELICOPTER - DAY   103

      Crandall is flying in more men. Out in front of them, they
      can see the artillery and air strikes going, a ring of fire
      and smoke lashing into the air; the center of the ring, their
      destination, is like the mouth of hell. Over the radio they
      hear the jumble of radio traffic, in the fight--

                    RADIO VOICES
          --We're taking fire, taking fire!
          --Get those sons-of-bitches
          --The Lieutenant's down!...

Crandall looks at Mills. No man could be called a coward for
refusing to go into that. Mills points at another section of
helicopters circling in the distance.

                    CRANDALL
               (into radio)
          First of the 7th Medevac wing, are you
          inbound?

                    MEDEVAC PILOT (ON RADIO)
          Looks pretty hot down there.

                    CRANDALL
          You can make it. Watch our approach, and
          follow us in.

                    MEDEVAC PILOT (ON RADIO)
          I don't know...

                    CRANDALL
          Hey, we're in the front, they'll all be
          shooting at us!

The Medevac choppers slide in behind Crandall's. Crandall
leads his section of choppers roaring in at treetop level
drawing enemy fire.

104   EXT. THE LANDING ZONE - DAY   104

Suddenly the clearing turns red hot with attacking North
Vietnamese. As the helicopters touch down, the NVA are
firing at the choppers point blank, from just outside the
length of the rotor blades.

Crandall and the others are swarmed by enemy bullets. One of
the group of soldiers in his choppers is shot in the head,
two more are wounded. Moore and his men already on the
ground race over and start cutting down the attackers. The
wounded Captain (Lefebvre) and his new cavalrymen pile out
from the choppers.

Crandall pulls pitch and lifts off. One of the Hueys behind
him gets hit by groundfire; bullets tear through the cockpit
and chop the control stick free. The copilot tries to steer
and is shot; the helicopter crash lands.

Over his radio, Crandall hears the Medevac leader--

                    MEDEVAC PILOT (ON RADIO)
              Pull out, it's too hot!

Crandall sees them veer off, abandoning the wounded lying on the ground. Crandall veers back to the LZ and lands again, shouting--

                    CRANDALL
              Give us the wounded!

They start piling the wounded aboard Crandall's chopper.

Metsker is one of the wounded, his shoulder bleeding through the bandages; but as he sees the helicopters filling up, he gives up his place to another man.

                    METSKER
              You go, I'll wait for the next flight!

They lift the other man on board, and Metsker stays behind, helped back toward the termite mound by Moore, as Crandall rams his throttle and gets the chopper airborne.

105   INT. CRANDALL'S CHOPPER - DAY   105

It's chaos, the gunners firing furiously, raking the trees, while the copilot, Mills, sees to the wounded crew chief.

                    CRANDALL
              Damn, those little bastards can shoot!

Crandall sees the Medevac choppers in the distance, retreating from the landing zone. He gets onto the radio, and speaks in an official voice.

                    CRANDALL (cont'd)
                (into radio)
              Can you patch me through to Medevac
              command, please?
                (beat)
              Medevac Command? This is Major Bruce
              Crandall, air wing, 7th Cavalry. I just
              wanted to say...FUCK YOU!

106   EXT. LANDING ZONE - DAY   106

Charlie Company is in a shit storm. Their captain, Bob Edwards, is racing down his line of firing soldiers as the reinforcements arrive.

                    EDWARDS
              They're still trying to flank us!
              Stretch out along the line!

They lie down in the tree line at the edge of the LZ. Dozens of NVA are coming at them.

                    EDWARDS (cont'd)
               (into radio)
          We are in heavy contact. In danger of
          being overrun! Damn! These guys are
          good!

107 INTERCUT AS NECESSARY, MOORE on the radio to Edwards.   107

                    MOORE
               (into radio)
          If they get into the LZ, we've had it.
          Can you hold?

                    EDWARDS (ON RADIO)
          All I've got holding my flank is one gun
          team!

108 EXT. ON THE ATTACK TRAILS OF THE MOUNTAIN - DAY   108

North Vietnamese are still streaming down.

109 EXT. ON THE ISOLATED FLANK - DAY   109

Beck and Adams are working their machine gun, Adams firing, Beck assisting, laying down sheets of machine-gun fire wreaking havoc on the attacking enemy. Beck spots an arm, off to his left about twenty yards, reaching up above the grass with a GI canteen in hand.

                    BECK
          Cover me, Russell!

Adams covers Beck with fire, and he runs over to find a wounded American, with a hole in his chest.

                    BECK (cont'd)
          Medic!

No Medic comes, and the NVA is closing on them. Beck grabs the wounded soldier's M-16 and tries to fire it, but the weapon has been damaged and falls apart in his hands. He drags the soldier through the firing, back to a spot where the medic gets to him.

Beck is running back toward Adams when Adams goes down, shot in the head. Beck reaches Adams. Adams is on his back staring up at Beck, the M-60 on the ground next to him. One side of Adams' head is a mess; he's trying to talk but nothing is coming out. The NVA knows they have him and is closing in on the front and right, from thirty yards out.

Beck rights the M-60 fast and starts firing at them. Every time he fires, Adams winces.

Suddenly the M-60 jams, with the enemy running at Beck. He flips it over and bangs it on the ground; the jammed shells fall loose; he flips it right side up, slaps the ammo belt back in, slams the feed cover closed and begins firing again. It seems like a lifetime--we do it in SLOW MOTION-- but it takes five or ten seconds. He turns and catches the attacking soldiers chest high with a stream of bullets from the M-60 machine gun.

The enemy firing slacks off; Beck sees Adams' helmet laying in front of him; he can see a bullet hole in it, and blood; he turns it over; what seems like Adams' entire brain falls out in front of him on the ground.

> BECK (cont'd)
> Medic! ...It's gonna be alright, Russ, it ain't nothin'... the choppers'll get you out... Medic!

Beck looks at the other gun crew; they've stopped firing because one of the gunners is hit. Just then the Medic moves up to help Russell Adams.

Beck watches as the Medic drags Adams away; then he sees that the gunner is dragging his partner back to the rear. Beck is alone, and the NVA are coming.

He picks up the M-60 again, and starts firing.

110   EXT. CRANDALL'S HELICOPTERS IN THE AIR - DAY   110

In formation, shot up, going as fast as they can go, full of wounded.

AT THE CONTROLS, Crandall hammers at the throttle.

> CRANDALL
> Those guys are fighting for their lives, and bleeding to death, and those chickenshits won't come help!

111   EXT. LZ X-RAY - THE TERMITE MOUND - DAY   111

Moore's gaze whips around the periphery of the LZ; they're fighting on three sides. He snaps another order.

> MOORE
> I want an emergency LZ carved out right there. Blow the trees down!

A team of engineers who came in with the reinforcements run across the ten yards of ground and start tying charges against the tree trunks; bullets drop two of the engineers as they work.

112　EXT. AIR CAV BASE - PLEI ME - DAY　112

Crandall drops his Huey, loaded with casualties, onto the ground at Plei Me. They're met by medics and troops still waiting to be lifted into X-Ray. The troops help remove the dead and wounded. Crandall hears -

> MOORE'S VOICE
> (over radio)
> Crandall, I'm closing the LZ! It's too hot to get you in here!

Crandall switches frequencies and radios Too Tall.

> CRANDALL
> Too Tall! Shut down! Load two Hueys with all the ammo they can carry. And get the rest of the pilots over here.

The huge black enlisted man, who stayed behind, wearing only G.I. shorts and boots, is reaching into the helicopter to pick up one of the dead white soldiers; it's the soldier who gave him the puppy. Tears are streaming down his face; he tenderly cradles that dead soldier to his chest and walks slowly from the aircraft to the medical station, as the puppy follows, whining its grief.

Lieutenant Jack Geoghegan and some of his Air Cav troopers are assembled nearby, waiting their turn to be ferried into the fight on the helicopters whose floors are slick with blood. Geoghegan moves to Crandall.

> GEOGHEGAN
> Sir, you gotta get us in there.

> CRANDALL
> I'm all for that, but I can't let you die getting there.

Too Tall returns with the rest of Crandall's pilots; they gather to him, and Crandall tells them--

> CRANDALL (cont'd)
> They need water, they need the wounded out, but they need ammo more than anything. I'm gonna take back two loads. It's redhot at the LZ.
> (MORE)

                    CRANDALL (cont'd)
          One bullet, one piece of shrapnel, and we
          turn into a burst of sunshine. I want
          volunteers.

                    TOO TALL
          Fuck volunteers, you want the best pilot,
          don't you?

                    CRANDALL
          Too Tall, you big stubborn son-of-a--
          Hell. We'll both do it.

113   INT. A SAIGON WAR ROOM   113

      Intelligence types--both uniformed and in plain clothes--are
      sweating and smoking in a radio-filled warm room. A
      DIPLOMATIC SPOOK in plain clothes is chain-smoking.

                    DIPLOMATIC SPOOK
          I don't like this. First time out, a
          whole battalion massacred.

                    ARMY INTELLIGENCE OFFICER
          You think this is a massacre?

                    DIPLOMATIC SPOOK
          I think losing a load of draftees is a
          bad week. Losing a Colonel is a
          massacre.

                    ARMY INTELLIGENCE OFFICER
          But Moore's still fighting.

                    DIPLOMATIC SPOOK
          He's under strength, against more men
          than he can count. He's got a whole
          patrol lost--

                    ARMY INTELLIGENCE OFFICER
          They're not lost. They're just cut off
          and surrounded.

                    DIPLOMATIC SPOOK
          Then they're lost.

      The two men arguing look toward the ranking officer, a
      General sitting in the shadows, his face lined with worry.

114   EXT. AIR CAV BASE - PLEI ME - DAY   114

      TWO CHOPPERS loaded with ammo struggle into the air.

INTERCUT AS NECESSARY, Crandall at the controls of one Huey, and Too Tall flying another. The radio is alive with shouts and screams of a desperate fight. Crandall breaks in--

>**CRANDALL**
>(into radio)
>Colonel, this is Snakeshit, we have two full loads of ammo.

115 INTERCUT AS NECESSARY, MOORE IN THE LANDING ZONE 115

with bullets cutting the air, and the enemy so close that Plumley and others around Moore are firing at NVA running at them from the surrounding treeline.

>**MOORE (ON RADIO)**
>Snake, it's hot down here. But we need that ammo.

116   **CRANDALL** 116
>Then we're coming.

VARIOUS SHOTS - CRANDALL'S SUICIDE MISSION

Crandall's chopper is in the lead, with Too Tall's right behind. As Crandall starts the approach, heavy groundfire rips into his helicopter.

>**CRANDALL**
>Too Tall, we're taking heavy groundfire!

117   **TOO TALL** 117
>(into radio)
>What do you want me to do about it, Snake? I kinda thought this might happen.

118 EXT. LZ X-RAY - AT THE TERMITE MOUND - DAY 118

As Plumley stands behind Moore, shielding him with his body and gunning down the individual NVA who've broken through, Moore is on the radio with Crandall.

>**MOORE**
>Approach from the east, Snake!

Metsker, fighting off the pain of his shoulder wound, is manning a radio.

>**METSKER**
>Colonel, it's Brigade headquarters! They want you out!

                    MOORE
          What?-- They...what? We can't get out!

                    METSKER
          Not all of us, just you. Saigon wants to
          debrief you!

Moore can't deal with this nonsense; he sees Crandall and his
helicopters coming in--and sees the enemy bullets cutting
through the grass at the spot where they're about to land.
Moore runs out into the enemy fire, waving to Crandall to set
the choppers down at the emergency LZ he's had the engineers
clear, where the firing is not so intense.

                    MOORE
          Over there, Snake! Over there!

119   IN THE CHOPPER   119

Crandall sees a man below him, waving.

120   TOO TALL   120
               (into radio)
          Snakeshit, you see that?

                    CRANDALL
          It's the Colonel! He wants us to land
          away from the trees.

They swing their choppers to earth where Moore is directing,
near the termite mound and the collection of wounded.

121   ON THE GROUND   121

the chopper crews toss off crates of ammo. Moore looks at
Crandall; Crandall, sitting in the bubble of the helicopter,
has a ringside seat of the desperation of the battle; he can
see NVA swarming right out of the trees, not thirty feet
away; they run toward the choppers, firing, and Moore cuts
them down. Crandall looks again at Moore; both understand
that these may be the last moments of their lives.

                    MOORE
          Get the wounded on! Tom, come on!

His shout is to his friend Metsker, who has been trying to
function in spite of his shattered shoulder. Metsker is in
great pain, but is helping Moore and the medics lift the
severely wounded onto the choppers...

Doc Carrara carries a wounded Captain (Lefebvre) up on a
stretcher; he's gravely wounded, and we see, from HIS POV,
the chaos and danger of the situation of the wounded...

Men shouting, the chopper blades turning above, the chopper crews screaming and loading on the wounded while they fire at the enemy in the trees.

> DOC CARRARA
> Got another one!

> CHOPPER CREW
> We're overloaded! Leave him!

But Metsker, about to step onto the chopper himself, turns and sees that the Captain is severly injured with blood gushing out of his right arm. Still from the Captain's POV, we see Metsker stop and turn back.

> METSKER
> No. He's a lot worse than me!

Metsker helps lift the Captain on--and suddenly jerks slightly, his face freezing... Metsker falls into the chopper; the crewmen drag him aboard as they lift away, leaving Moore behind, standing in the hail of gunfire.

122 EXT. MOORE'S COMMAND POST - DAY   122

Moore goes to the pile of gear taken from the wounded and fills his ammo pouches and pockets, grabs extra grenades, jacks a fresh magazine into his M-16, and says to Plumley--

> MOORE
> You, me and Ouellette are the only
> reserve we have left.

Plumley loads his pockets too. But then he notices...

> PLUMLEY
> It's slackin' up a little.

> MOORE
> They're regrouping for another assault.
> Distribute the ammo. And tell Crandall
> we can get one more flight in here.

As Ouellette gets on the radio to repeat the order, his mouth is so dry he can't speak. Moore gives him a drink from his canteen, then hands the canteen to Plumley.

> MOORE (CONT'D)
> Give it to the wounded. Everybody's out
> of water, it must be terrible for them...

He looks in the direction of the cut-off platoon.

MOORE (cont'd)
...And for those guys cut off out there.

123 EXT. THE CUT-OFF PLATOON - DAY   123

The platoon clings to its tiny, tortured piece of earth, as
NVA troopers probe at their position. The cut-off platoon
survivors bang away at men running at them from every
direction.

Three enemy soldiers have crawled through the grass until
they are almost on top of the Americans; now they rise
suddenly from the ground right in front of Ernie Savage.
Savage jumps upright in surprise and swings his M-16 toward
them, only to realize that his rifle is empty.

For an instant eternity, Savage doesn't know what to do. So
he smiles and says cheerfully--

                    SAVAGE
          Hi!

All three look at him in momentary confusion; by then he has
slipped in a fresh magazine and sprayed them. Savage drops
back to the ground, shouting--

                    SAVAGE (cont'd)
          They're crawling up on us! Put your guns
          flat on the ground and lay the fire into
          them two or three inches high!

The Americans do just that, firing along the ground, all
around them. Then they cease fire, and hear the MOANS of
wounded enemy in the grass; they fire again, stop--and hear
nothing but the fighting two hundred yards away.

                    SAVAGE (cont'd)
          We better burn the codes.

They collect maps, notebooks, and signal operating
instructions booklets from the dead commanders and Savage
burns them all, as he and his small band hunker down,
determined to hold their ground to the end.

124 EXT. THE LZ - DAY   124

Choppers are landing two at a time; drawing fire...

125 INT. A CHOPPER AS IT LANDS   125

Jack Geoghegan is one of the new troopers riding into the
battle;

the door gunners are firing back at the NVA, and enemy bullets are already zinging around Geoghegan and his men. Geoghegan unbuckles as the chopper drops toward the ground; he readies his M-16 and leaps out before the skids touch, leading his men across the open field, under fire, shooting at enemy on the ground and in the trees overhead.

126 EXT. LZ X-RAY - BY THE TERMITE MOUND - DAY   126

Geoghegan reaches Moore at his command post.

> GEOGHEGAN
> Colonel.

Geoghegan's blood is up from the run across the field, the sudden plunge into battle, but he is clear-eyed and steady. Moore looks at this young brave man, with the fresh clean face, not yet stained with the fight. For a moment the earnest, innocent, youthfulness of that face reminds Moore of all the young lives at stake in this battle. Then--

> MOORE
> Get over with your Company.

Moore points toward the most desperate spot in the line, where Edwards' men have been battling the fiercest assaults.

> GEOGHEGAN
> Yes sir.

Moore watches as Geoghegan rushes across the open, bullet-riddled landing zone, leading his men to the hottest spot on the perimeter.

At that same moment more CHOPPERS ARE LANDING, with more troopers, including a weapons platoon with mortars. The soldiers pile out with their heavy weapons, and Moore runs to meet them.

BETWEEN THE CHOPPERS AND THE TERMITE MOUND

Moore reaches the officer of the mortar platoon.

> MOORE
> Set the mortars up here!

As the mortar crews start forming a firing pit near the termite hill, Moore takes the radio handset.

> MOORE (cont'd)
> Captain Nadal--we've got to get to that cut-off platoon.

127 EXT. THE DRY CREEKBED - DAY   127

>   Nadal's platoon leaders are with him as he draws formations
>   in the dirt, like a football play in a sandlot game.
>
>   NADAL
>   We'll use an echelon left. All right...
>   That's an American platoon, an Air Cav
>   platoon, cut off out there and we're
>   gonna go after them! Air Cav! Air Cav!
>
>   TROOPERS
>   Air Cav! Air Cav! Air Cav!
>
>   Nadal stands and gives the signal. He leads his men in a
>   charge out of the creekbed, into the brush and trees between
>   them and the cut-off platoon.
>
>   Nadal and his men are immediately met by a storm of North
>   Vietnamese running at them.
>
>   A machine gun burst sweeps across the Americans; all of them
>   are diving for cover, except Nadal; he's trying to charge
>   forward when the umbilical cord of his phone pulls him back
>   and he realizes his radio operator and the other two men with
>   him have all been cut down. Nadal dives to the earth and
>   grabs his radio.
>
>   NADAL
>   It's a shitstorm, Colonel! Looks like
>   they launched an assault at exactly the
>   time we launched ours.

128 INTERCUT AS NECESSARY, MOORE AT THE TERMITE MOUND   128

>   on his radio, taking the bad news in stride.
>
>   MOORE
>   Pull back to the creekbed, and hold.
>
>   NADAL
>   Roger that, Sir.
>
>   Nadal signals his men to retreat, and leads them toward the
>   shelter of the creekbed.
>
>   From the creekbed, Nadal's men join a growing stream of
>   walking wounded flowing back toward the battalion aid
>   station, as the sun has dropped behind the massif and night
>   is falling.

129   EXT. AIR CAV BASE - PLEI ME - DUSK   129

The sun is disappearing behind the horizon as Crandall sets
his chopper down, along with seven others, in front of the
last contingent of men and supplies ready to be flown into
the battle. A stocky journalist runs up to shout to him,
over the hack of the rotors. It's JOE GALLOWAY, a 23-year-
old reporter with cameras dangling from his neck.

                    GALLOWAY
            Room for me?

                    CRANDALL
            If you're crazy enough, get in!

130   INT. HELICOPTER - SUNDOWN   130

The helicopter lifts as Galloway piles in; he's thrilled to
be going; then he sees that he's sitting on a pile of ammo
and grenades. Oh shit. The bullet holes all over the
chopper aren't comforting either.

THEY FLY INTO THE GROWING DARKNESS; Galloway leans to
Crandall and points down to the dark ground.

                    GALLOWAY
            What is that?

Far below they see a stream of lights moving down the Chu
Pong Massif.

                    CRANDALL
            Enemy soldiers. They use candles on the
            trail. They're moving into position to
            attack.

It's a sickening sight, how many there are.

                    CRANDALL (cont'd)
            Here we go...

The ride in is heart-stopping: down into the darkness,
clipping the tree tops, the big slow target taking fire from
every NVA sniper in the area. The men pile out, the crewmen
heaving ammo and five-gallon jugs of water into the grass.

131   EXT. LZ X-RAY - DUSK   131

It is fast growing dark within the clearing. Moore watches
the helicopter as medics quickly reload it with wounded--
Adams among them--and he speaks on the radio to Crandall,
whom he can see in the cockpit.

MOORE
You and your boys have done a hell of a
job today, Snake.

CRANDALL (ON RADIO)
Last flight til dawn, Colonel. But you
need us, you call. We do home
deliveries, night or day.

Crandall takes off into the darkness, green tracers from
enemy fire slashing past his chopper. As it lifts away,
Moore sees that someone has gotten off. It's Galloway.

He runs up. All the soldiers--Plumley, Ouellette, Moore--
look at him like they can't believe he's there.

GALLOWAY
Joe Galloway, reporter for U.P.I. How's
it goin', Colonel?

MOORE
My men are into their second straight
night without sleep. And we're greatly
outnumbered.

GALLOWAY
With more enemy coming, Sir. We just saw
a whole chain of lights, moving down the
mountain.

MOORE
I can't guarantee your safety.

GALLOWAY
I know.

MOORE
Where you from, son?

GALLOWAY
Refugio Texas, sir.

MOORE
Well...that's the only thing that's made
sense all day. ...Let's get some
artillery fire onto those lights!

Moore walks away. Galloway, left alone, looks around at the
dangerous darkness.

132 EXT. CAMP HOLLOWAY - NIGHT   132

Beneath a makeshift shelter made of ponchos, lit by red-lens flashlights, the surgeons are working frantically, squeezing blood bags to pump blood into the wounded and tie off the injured arteries and veins.

Beside the MASH unit is another open shelter, where Graves Registration workers are checking dogtags and identifying the dead, for notification of next of kin, again under the eerie glow of red-lens flashlights.

Crandall's and Too Tall's choppers, heavily loaded with wounded, touch down outside the MASH unit. As the wounded are being off-loaded, Crandall spots the medevac pilot who refused to fly into the LZ. They avert their eyes; but one of them, their COMMANDING OFFICER, glares at Crandall.

Crandall's hand shakes as he reaches to the switch that shuts down his chopper. It is a sudden, unexpected SILENCE as the blades stop for the first time all day.

The maintenance crews move to his chopper, and stop-- appalled. The floor of the helicopter is covered in blood.

Crandall can barely get out of his seat, he's been in it so long. He stands, and takes a step out. But he's shaking violently. His legs give way. He drops to his knees. And he begins to vomit.

                    VOICE
          Crandall!

Crandall stands to face the medevac commanding officer, storming up to him.

                    MEDEVAC COMMANDING OFFICER
          You led my people into a hot LZ!

                    CRANDALL
          Somebody had to fly out the wounded.

                    MEDEVAC COMMANDING OFFICER
          Don't play hotshot with me! You know the
          rules! You suckered us! And I'm warning
          you, don't ever do it again, or I'll have
          you busted!

                    CRANDALL
          You've got the balls to face me, but not
          the balls to face the enemy?

Crandall goes for his pistol, and means to use it. Too Tall grabs for Crandall, and the Medevac Officer runs for cover.

                    CRANDALL (cont'd)
     I ever see you again, I'll kill you!

Too Tall hangs on til Crandall quits struggling; then...

                    TOO TALL
     Quite a day.

                    CRANDALL
     Tomorrow will be worse. If they make it
     to tomorrow.

133   EXT. THE CUT-OFF PLATOON - NIGHT   133

Savage and the others are pressed to the ground, where they've scratched out foxholes as best they can--slight depressions in the hard earth. It's quiet; they whisper--

                    BUNGUM
       (terrified)
     Ernie, it's pitch black, I can't see
     anything.

                    SAVAGE
       (into radio)
     Illumination, nine-three-one, zero-one-
     four.

An illumination shell, fired from the artillery battery miles away, explodes above them and lights up the sky. They see silhouettes--men moving toward them.

The Americans start shooting--and the flashes of their guns help give them light. The NVA blow BUGLES and run at them in a full-on charge.

The Americans, just a dozen men lying on a little rise of earth, fire carefully, as Savage shouts coordinates into his radio, over the sudden crash of noise.

                    SAVAGE (cont'd)
     Nine-three-two, zero-one-five!...

Savage keeps the radio in one hand and uses his M-16 with the other to shoot down two NVA almost on top of them.

The artillery rains in. Between it and the rifle fire, the NVA are beaten back. Savage yells--

                    SAVAGE (cont'd)
          Save your ammo! Cease fire!
          Anybody hit?

The men are wild-eyed with terror, Bungum hyperventilating.

                    BUNGUM
          Ernie...

                    SAVAGE
          We're gonna make it. Stay down, and save
          your ammo. We're gonna make it.

Savage lifts the radio, and speaks softly, hopefully...

                    SAVAGE (cont'd)
          Captain, it's dark out here... So if you
          guy's are coming, better let us know so
          we don't shoot any of our own guys.

134   INTERCUT - MOORE'S COMMAND POST, NADAL AND MOORE listening   134
      to this; they've been trying to figure a way to get to them
      tonight; Nadal answers, struggling to be positive...

                    NADAL
               (into radio)
          Savage...we can't make it tonight.

135   THE CUT-OFF PLATOON - The others are looking at Savage--and   135
      they know what he's hearing. And none of them believe
      there's any way they can hang on through the night.

                    NADAL (ON RADIO) (CONT'D)
          ...But don't worry, you'll make it.
          You've already won this fight. We'll get
          to you in the morning.

                    SAVAGE
          Yes sir.

Savage signs off.

                    BUNGUM
          We're dead. We're all dead.

                    SAVAGE
          We can make it, if we can hold out
          through the night. Just keep cool. Bear
          down. We'll make it.

136 EXT. CHARLIE COMPANY PERIMETER - NIGHT   136

Geoghegan and the others have dug in. All around, they watch the falling darkness, and the ominous silence.

MOORE AND PLUMLEY walk the perimeter. Men who feel defeated suddenly perk up as their Colonel joins them on the line.

     MOORE
  Great job today, men.

A soldier turns and smiles; it's Geoghegan.

     GEOGHEGAN
  They won't get through us, sir.

Ouellette is on the radio; he hands Moore the handset.

     OUELLETTE
  Rear Headquarters, Sir.

137   RADIO VOICE   137
  How is it out there, Colonel?

     MOORE
  We are surrounded but we are holding. I
  want a confirmed count of our dead and
  wounded.

     RADIO VOICE
  You'll get it, Hal.

     MOORE
  I need that count.

Moore hangs up. He sees a full moon rising. He pauses for a moment, thinking of Julie. Just then Geoghegan tenses.

     GEOGHEGAN
  Here they come.

     GODBOLDT
  Here who comes?

     PLUMLEY
  Who the hell do you think? Illumination!

A flare pops overhead, lighting NVA moving through the darkness. The Americans on the line open fire, and suddenly the enemy comes swarming toward their line.

138   INT. MOORE'S HOUSE, LIVING ROOM - FT. BENNING - DAY   138

   Julie is vacuuming; when she shuts off the vacuum motor she
   hears a wail of grief coming from the house next door. She
   looks out and sees a yellow cab pulling away; the crying
   continues...

139   EXT. NEIGHBOR'S HOUSE - DAY   139

   Julie moves up and knocks on the door. Catherine opens it,
   shattered, holding the telegram. Julie knows from the look
   on her face exactly what it is.

   Julie moves inside; Catherine is awash in shock and grief.

                       CATHERINE
             A telegram!... A telegram! A cab
             delivers a telegram! The Secretary of
             the Army regrets--

   She can't go further. Julie hurts as if the telegram was
   hers, and in a way it is. Catherine pulls back, struggling
   to gain control.

                       CATHERINE (cont'd)
             I need... I need to make some calls, I...

                       JULIE
             Let me help.

                       CATHERINE
             No, I-- need to do this alone.

                       JULIE
             I'll be next door.

   Catherine nods. Julie wants to help, and she has no words.

140   INT. MOORE'S HOUSE - FT. BENNING - DAY   140

   Julie walks in, nearly collapsing in the echo of Catherine's
   tragedy. And then there is a knock on the door. Julie looks
   out. Parked in front of her house is a yellow cab--and at
   the door is its driver. Through the curtains of the front
   door Julie can see that he holds a telegram in his hand.

   Panic sweeps through her body; she moves behind the window
   curtains and hides. The cab driver knocks again, the sound
   like thunder through her brain.

   She grabs at the vacuum and turns it on to try to drown the
   sound; he rings the doorbell.

She can't hide any longer; she switches off the vacuum and opens the door.

> CAB DRIVER
> Miz Moore?...Colonel Moore's wife?

Julie can only nod. He lifts the telegram.

> CAB DRIVER (cont'd)
> I need help finding an address...

> JULIE
> You...you stupid...JACKASS! YOU KNOW WHAT THIS IS!! DON'T YOU KNOW WHAT YOU JUST DID TO ME?!

The tears and anger are bursting through her eyes. He stares at her, and steps backward in shame. He's a veteran himself.

> CAB DRIVER
> I don't like this job. I'm just trying to do it.

He starts away.

> JULIE
> Wait.

She goes to him and takes the telegram. She sees the name, and winces with pain.

> JULIE (cont'd)
> I'll take it to her.

He nods his thanks and starts to get into his cab.

> JULIE (cont'd)
> And tell the cab company--if you get any others, just bring them to me.

141   EXT. TREE-LINED STREET - FT. BENNING - DAY   141

Julie walks down the street. Barbara Geoghegan, two doors down, is handing her baby to a neighbor and hurries to Julie.

> BARBARA
> Julie, I just went by to see Catherine.

As Julie keeps walking, Barbara looks at the telegram in her hand.

                    BARBARA (cont'd)
          No chaplains or counselors, just cab
          drivers.

                    JULIE
          The Army wasn't ready.

                    BARBARA
          I'll go with you.

They head up a walkway to a door; they knock. The door
opens, and a woman sees them, her face realizing...

142   EXT. TREE-LINED STREET - FT. BENNING - DAY   142

Julie and Barbara, wrung out from their mission, walk slowly
back toward Julie's.

                    JULIE
          I was afraid...she would hate me.

                    BARBARA
          Because your husband's the leader?
               (beat)
          He didn't start the war, Julie. And he
          didn't make 'em go. They all knew this
          could happen. So did we.

As they draw close to the Moore's house, they see a cab
pulling away. With fear slowing their steps, they move down
the walk. On the porch by the front door is a stack of
twenty more telegrams.

Julie and Barbara are frozen. Julie lifts them, like a jar
of poison.

                    JULIE
          I'll do this.

                    BARBARA
          No, I'll help you.

                    JULIE
          We'll do one at a time. We won't look,
          okay?

                    BARBARA
          Okay...

Julie stuffs them into her purse, then, stiffening herself to
the task, she reaches in and withdraws a telegram, reading
the addressee name with sadness...

                    JULIE
               Sally Lane...

     MONTAGE - BRINGING THE NEWS...

143 EXT. A FRONT STOOP - DAY   143

     Julie and Barbara leave the home of one of the new widows.
     They stand out on the porch, and take a deep breath. Julie
     pulls another telegram from her purse...

                    JULIE
               Alice Gray...

     They move off again.

144 IN SLOW DISSOLVES we see the same thing happen twice   144
     more...and come out of the montage on

145 ANOTHER FRONT PORCH, as Julie lifts the last envelope.   145

                    JULIE (cont'd)
               The last one. Jo Ann Brown.

     They both feel guilty relief...then move on.

146 EXT. GEOGHEGAN'S HOUSE - DAY   146

     Julie and Barbara, finished now, stop outside Barbara's
     house.

                    BARBARA
               Julie? You think there'll be more
               telegrams tomorrow?
                    (beat)
               If there are...come get me.

147 EXT. LZ X-RAY, BEHIND THE COMMAND POST - NIGHT   147

     The overworked medical group is struggling to keep a dozen
     wounded alive. Doc Carrara looks up from the wounded trooper
     he's working on, to see Moore standing there.

                    DOC CARRARA
               A dozen wounded we couldn't get out...

                    MOORE
               Crandall will be back in the morning.
               How many bodies still here?

                    DOC CARRARA
               At least two dozen.

Doc nods toward the space behind the medical area, where two dozen bodies lie neatly on the ground, the moonlight glancing off the ponchos that cover them.

Moore moves out among them. So many--and more, many more, back at the base camp. Young men he led; young lives, and early deaths, and he led them here.

Moore says a silent prayer. Then he becomes aware of Galloway moving up to him.

                MOORE
    You have a death wish, Galloway?

                GALLOWAY
    No sir.

                MOORE
    Then why did you come?

                GALLOWAY
    Because I knew they would be here.

He means the dead Americans. Moore looks at him for a long moment, and then looks away, across the rows of dead soldiers in their ponchos.

                MOORE
    How come you're not a soldier, Joe?
    You've got the guts for it.

                GALLOWAY
    I come from a long line of soldiers. My
    daddy. My grand-daddy. Two of my great
    grand-daddies were soldiers--hell, it's
    how I came to be. They each lost a leg
    in the Civil War: great-granddaddy
    Galloway lost his left, and great-
    granddaddy Reid lost his right. They met
    in a shoe store in Galveston--and then
    met once a year every year after, on the
    same date, in the same store, to pick out
    one new pair of shoes for the two of
    them. One had a daughter, one had a son--
    my grandparents.

Moore does something he didn't think he could do on this night: he smiles.

                GALLOWAY (cont'd)
    Galloways have been in every war this
    country has ever fought. When it came to
    this one...
                (MORE)

                    GALLOWAY (cont'd)
          well I didn't figure I could stop a war,
          but I thought I might try to understand
          one. And I could do it better aiming a
          camera than I could aiming a rifle.

Moore looks out over the dead soldiers again.

                    MOORE
          I hope you live through this one.

Moore starts to walk away.

                    GALLOWAY
          Colonel? ...I hope you do too.

Moore looks at him, and moves back to the Command Post.

148 INT. COLONEL AHN'S UNDERGROUND BUNKER - NIGHT   148

     Colonel Ahn has gathered his top officers together; twenty
     men, clear-eyed and professional. They are like the home
     team huddled in the locker room at half time, when the game
     is going their way. Ahn is positive, intense, direct.

                    AHN
          We fought well today. We tested their
          tactics and learned their capabilities.
          Their artillery is effective, so we must
          get so close they can't use it. We will
          grab them by the belt buckle.

149 EXT. THE CUT-OFF PLATOON, ON THE LITTLE KNOLL - NIGHT   149

     The patrol on the knoll is even more alone in the darkness,
     as the enemy moves in around them, firing tracers. Savage is
     shouting into the radio, calling in artillery.

                    SAVAGE
          Right twenty!

Fragmentation shells burst behind the charging enemy.

                    BUNGUM
          Closer, Ernie!

                    SAVAGE
               (into radio)
          Right twenty more!

Artillery rounds scream in, leveling the attackers. Two
shells fall almost on top of the Americans, the blasts
bouncing them off the ground. Savage and Bungum keep their
faces buried as spent shrapnel clatters down around them.
Then they lift their heads gingerly.

                        SAVAGE (cont'd)
            Close enough?

      They hear the bugles again; the NVA charge, through the
      night.

150   MONTAGE - THE CUT-OFF PLATOON'S LAST STAND   150

      It is an image out of the great heroic portraits of battle,
      and it is real: Savage and the rest of the cut-off platoon
      make their stand, a circle of men surrounded on a small round
      knoll. Their dead are lying within their circle; their
      wounded have their weapons bound into their hands with
      bandages and toilet paper; and even their medic, Charlie
      Lose, wounded twice already, is fighting.

      The bravery of the North Vietnamese is just as striking.
      They run through artillery blasts that shatter most of their
      comrades--and yet their numbers are so great that many of
      them reach the American circle, where they are met with rifle
      fire, and grenades, and pistol shots, and bayonets.

      OVER THIS, we hear the sound of the hymns from the Southern
      churches, singing like prayers...and DISSOLVE TO LATER...

      The field around the knoll is littered with North Vietnamese
      dead. We PAN them and reach the cut-off platoon...still
      there.

      Now it is so black they can't see. Ernie and the others lie
      there, terrified. Silence. No water, their lips parched.
      One of the wounded croaks for water.

      Medic Lose crawls to him, and tries to keep him quiet. All
      the men are terrified.

      Savage, lying filthy and dust-covered, is straining to hear;
      is something out there? It's so dark he can see nothing but
      the stars in the sky. Then he sees a silhouette, blotting
      out stars; an enemy soldier is moving up. Bungum sees it
      too; his eyes go wide with terror.

      They see another figure, and another... It's a whole North
      Vietnamese patrol, advancing through the darkness. But they
      don't see the Americans, who are so filthy and covered with
      dirt from the artillery barrages that they blend right in
      with the ground, especially in this darkness.

      The whole enemy patrol walks right among the Americans!
      Savage slips the safety off his rifle...CLICK. The NVA hear
      it, but before they can react Savage opens fire; he and the
      other Americans spray the NVA.

All the NVA are dead, but a couple of the wounded Americans are moaning with pain and fear.

>   SAVAGE
>   Quiet, you'll get us killed!

The moaning doesn't stop.

>   SAVAGE (cont'd)
>   Look! We've made it!

He points to the horizon. The first pink rays of dawn appear in the east. They've lasted the night. The troopers stop crying.

151   SAME TIME - EXT. LZ X-RAY - MOORE'S COMMAND POST   151

Moore, holding his M-16, is crouched on the ground with Plumley, Nadal, and two other Captains.

>   MOORE
>   We'll attack with three companies in a
>   wedge formation. Move off from the creek
>   bed and go hard and fast til we reach the
>   knoll. Make sure Savage knows--I don't
>   want any Americans shooting each other.

>   NADAL
>   Who do you want at the point?

>   MOORE
>   I'm leading the assault. Dillon, you're
>   in charge of the LZ.

DILLON, a brave but young officer, is hesitant...

>   DILLON
>   Colonel... This is the nerve center of
>   the whole battle. Didn't you tell us
>   when a commander jumps into a fight he
>   becomes just another rifleman?

>   MOORE
>   Yeah. I also trained you to do my job.
>   Those are my men out there, and I'm going
>   to get them.

Moore leads his men across the landing zone, keeping low because sniper fire is already cutting the pink air of dawn.

152   EXT. NEAR THE CREEK BED - DAWN   152

Moore and his men reach a position by the creek bed; and then Moore stops, and listens.

                    NADAL
          What is it, Sir?

                    MOORE
          It's dead quiet. Nothing's wrong
          ...except that nothing's wrong.

                    OUELLETTE
          Maybe they've had enough.

                    MOORE
          They've walked through machine gun fire,
          artillery, and napalm. They're not gonna
          quit now.

He takes his radio, and calls Dillon at the Command Post.

                    MOORE (cont'd)
          Matt, have all companies send recon
          patrols forward of their positions.

153   EXT. AMERICAN PERIMETER - NEAR THE TREE LINE - DAWN   153

Scouting parties of Americans, three or four men in each party, begin to move forward carefully, through the tall grass and the trees... Geoghegan leads one group. We follow Geoghegan's group, who have moved ahead forty yards when--

HUNDREDS OF NORTH VIETNAMESE, their bodies camouflaged with grass and brush so that they blend right into the landscape, rise up from the earth and begin firing. Geoghegan and his men fall to the ground and start spraying fire from their M-16's; Geoghegan shouts into the radio--

                    GEOGHEGAN
          We have enemy attack! In force!

Geoghegan's men and the other recon platoons are fighting for their lives...

The Americans still dug in on the perimeter lay down a stream of fire, and artillery falls; all hell breaks loose.

154   EXT. AMERICAN PERIMETER - AT THE CREEKBED - DAWN   154

North Vietnamese boil up the same way attacking the creekbed, trying to overrun the landing zone from that direction too.

Moore and the group he's leading plunge into the fight, gunning down attackers with their M-16's.

Bill Beck slides into position with his M-60, and he and the other American gunners rake the swarms of attacking enemy with devastating fire, beating them back. Moore looks to the opposite side of the LZ; the intensity there is increasing, with bullets cutting through the clearing.

      MOORE
  They're attacking us from all sides. I
  gotta get back to the Command Post.

      PLUMLEY
  Soon as the shooting dies down we'll--

But Moore is already running through the fire; Plumley goes after him.

155 EXT. LZ X-RAY COMMAND POST - DAY   155

Moore and Plumley, bullets zinging around them, reach the command post; Dillon hands Moore a radio handset.

      DILLON
  It's Edwards!

156 INTERCUT - EXT. CHARLIE COMPANY PERIMETER - DAY 156

Captain Edwards is on the radio to Moore--and the attackers are swarming right to the edges of the fighting holes before they are cut down.

      EDWARDS
  They're inside the artillery! I need--

Edwards gets shot in the back. He falls face first.

157 MOORE, AT HIS COMMAND POST hears the rattle of gunfire from 157
  Edward's position, then nothing.

      MOORE
  Bob--? Bob?!--

The other end of the radio is dead.

Bullets are raking the LZ. It looks terrible now. Field medics are carrying wounded into the aid station behind the termite mound, where Doc Cararra and his two medics are already overwhelmed with the wounded, squeezing blood bags to get blood into a convulsing trooper, as Carrara works feverishly to tie off ruptured arteries.

Moore forces himself to concentrate, to keep his head. The noise of battle is unbelievable. Moore turns to Dillon and shouts over the noise--

                    MOORE (cont'd)
        Put the artillery right on the line! And
        order Bravo Company to send a platoon
        across the clearing to reinforce Charlie
        Company!

Dillon shouts into the radio, and on the far side of the clearing they see Bravo Company responding--seventeen troopers heading out in a low crouch, moving fast in short bounds across the open ground under heavy enemy automatic-weapons fire. Four of them go down.

The situation looks even worse. Terrified troopers drag their wounded and dead buddies into the aid station, screaming as they pass Moore--

                    TROOPERS
        We're being overrun!

                    MOORE
        Nah, boys, we're gonna win this fight.

Enemy fire from rifles and heavy machine guns shreds the elephant grass and sweeps over the battalion command post and aid station. Leaves, bark, and small branches flutter down on Moore and the others. NVA run into the LZ and Moore and his men cut them down.

158   EXT. AMONG THE NORTH VIETNAMESE TROOPS - DAY   158

A young North Vietnamese soldier crouches with his comrades amid the chaos of battle; but this particular soldier is in a certain kind of wide-eyed battle trance, like we saw in Ahn in the opening scene. As his comrades duck from the artillery, he leaps to his feet and begins to run through it.

We FOLLOW HIS RUN, past dead comrades, blasts of artillery, through the hand-to-hand fighting at the lines, the camera HIS POV as if the bayonet at the tip of his AK-47 were thrusting him forward. He penetrates the landing zone, and races across it...

HAL MOORE stands at the termite mound, his back to the charging NVA soldier. Plumley is firing at other NVA coming in from the side, and doesn't see this soldier...

Moore remains calm, the radio handset to his ear, and talks with forced calm.

                    MOORE
               (into radio)
          Colonel Brown, request you prepare
          another company of reinforcements for
          movement as soon as it can be
          accomplished without undue risk.

                    COLONEL BROWN (VOICE)
          Done. ...How bad is it, Hal?

     The young NVA rushes at Moore, closer...closer... At the last
     instant, Moore turns and fires directly into the lens--into
     the face of the onrushing soldier.

                    MOORE
          It's pretty sporty down here, Sir.

     Galloway passes Moore, carrying a wounded trooper, and
     deposits the man with the medics.

159 EXT. IN THE AIR, CRANDALL'S CHOPPERS - DAY   159

     Crandall is leading a flight of choppers toward the LZ, and
     it's looking worse than ever, explosions erupting in a circle
     of hell far below them.

                    CRANDALL
               (into radio)
          Hang on, Colonel, we're comin'!

160 EXT. LANDING ZONE - COMMAND POST - DAY   160

                    MOORE
               (into radio)
          Not yet, Snake, it's too hot!!

161 ON THE PERIMETER - DAY   161

     The fighting is ferocious; the NVA are reaching the foxholes,
     and much of the fighting is now hand-to-hand.

     Edwards is barely still alive, though shot in the back. He
     rolls over and finds his left arm won't work. He reaches for
     the radio, and calls--

162 MOORE AT THE COMMAND POST, under fire, hears Edwards.   162

                    EDWARDS (ON RADIO)
          They've penetrated, Colonel!

163 Dillon is on the other radio, and shouts to Moore--   163

                    DILLON
          They're hitting D-Company too! These are
          V.C., black uniforms, full battle gear!

Moore hears this report, and says to his team--

                    MOORE
          Now they've brought in a main force
          battalion of Viet Cong.

Nobody around Moore says anything; it's like they've just
heard their death sentence. An officer is trembling in death
throes at the termite mound. As he dies, Plumley takes his
.45 and shoves it into his belt. Moore is icy.

                    MOORE (cont'd)
          Sgt. Major, we can expect an attack on
          our rear.

164   JOE GALLOWAY   164

          lies in the middle of the landing zone, near the mortar crews
          who are firing furiously as their SERGEANT shouts--

                    MORTAR SERGEANT
          Straight up! They're right on top of us!

Galloway struggles to take pictures; he catches a few of a
young Japanese-American, who grins at the camera even as he
loads shells into the mortar tubes.

                    GALLOWAY
          What's your name?

                    NAKAYAMA
          Nakayama! I got a baby being born today!

As Galloway tries to note down the name, the man next to
Nakayama is shot; as Nakayama kneels over him to try to stop
the bleeding, the elephant grass comes alive, bullets
skimming two feet off the ground. Galloway hugs the earth,
terrified that to move anything would be to get it shot off.
Then he feels the toe of a combat boot jammed into his ribs,
and can't believe somebody is kicking him. He twists in
surprise to see Sgt. Major Plumley, all 6'2" of him standing
tall in the hail of gunfire.

                    PLUMLEY
          You can't take no pictures laying down
          there on the ground, Sonny.

Plumley is fearless--he's even grinning. Galloway, stunned, jumps up and for a comical moment he tries to take pictures, his hands shaking; but Plumley snatches him by the collar and pulls him back toward the aid station.

165   AT THE AID STATION   165

a bullet hits and kills the wounded man that Doc Carrara is working on. The Doc and medics realize they are about to be overrun. Plumley arrives with Galloway and positions him on the ground, takes the camera from him and shoves an extra rifle into his hands.

                        GALLOWAY
            But Sir...I'm a non-combatant.

                        PLUMLEY
            Ain't no such thing today, boy.

Galloway takes a position among the others. Bullets still sing overhead, but no one is firing at them just yet.

All the men look at Plumley, as he draws out his two .45 pistols, one in each hand, and cocks both.

                      PLUMLEY (cont'd)
            Gentlemen...prepare to defend yourselves.

The medics, the wounded, and Galloway especially, are wide-eyed at the moment. They scan the surrounding brush, trees, grass; they are at the rear of the perimeter, the place that has not been attacked in force since the battle began.

For a moment, they see nothing but brush, and hear nothing but the sound of the battle in other parts of the field.

And then they come: HUNDREDS OF NORTH VIETNAMESE, screaming, firing, charging toward the Americans.

Moore lowers the radio, steps up beside Plumley, and raises his M-16.

The Americans begin to fire. At first they just pour out a stream of bullets into the wave of NVA, but as their rifle magazines and pistol clips become exhausted and they must reload, their fire becomes sporadic, individual...

The NVA attack reaches the Americans... Moore sprays down a man, changes magazines, and sprays down another; Plumley shoots a man in the belly, another in the chest, another in the face... When he's swarmed he draws the second .45 and fires that too. The wounded Americans shoot...

And Galloway, the non-combatant, untrained for this job, yet committed to it now, fires too.

The fighting becomes a melee, all chaos and violence...

And the NVA are gone, lying dead all around, or crawling back the way they came, gut-shot, bleeding, dying.

166 EXT. AT THE TERMITE MOUND - DAY   166

Moore steps back to his command post, where Dillon and Hastings are hunkered down, feverishly working the radios. In the middle of all this, Moore senses something else--

                    MOORE
        Why aren't the mortar crews firing?

167 NEAR THE TERMITE HILL, BESIDE THE COMMAND POST   167

The mortar crews have ammo but are gripping the earth as bullets fly over them. Moore strides up to them.

                    MOORE
        What's wrong?

                MORTAR SERGEANT
        The tubes are red hot! We're gonna cook
        a round off inside the tubes and blow us
        all up! And we can't cool down the tubes
        cause we're outta water!

Moore turns to the mortar tubes; with bullets singing all around his head he opens his fly and starts pissing on a hot mortar tube. The stream of urine turns to steam...and cools the tube.

The mortar troops look at each other; they jump up and follow their Colonel's example, some pissing on the tubes while others feed shells and resume firing.

168 EXT. CHARLIE COMPANY LINE - DAY - OVERHEAD POV OF EDWARDS   168

Edwards has been wounded three times. He's lying next to a Lieutenant, ARRINGTON, who has taken a bullet in the chest.

                    ARRINGTON
        Captain...tell my wife I love her.

                    EDWARDS
        ...Don't you see I'm hit worse than you
        are, you dumb son-of-a-bitch?

Then Arrington realizes Edwards is right; the surprise, and Edward's response, seems to enliven them both.

169   QUICK PAN to Jack Geoghegan, nearby....   169

A shoulder-fired rocket hits the man next to him; Geoghegan sees the NVA close by.

> GEOGHEGAN
> They've got a rocket team behind that anthill!

> GODBOLDT
> The Captain and Arrington are both hit!

Geoghegan sees he's right; his POV scans the situation; it's up to him.

> GEOGHEGAN
> Cover me!

He charges out of the fighting hole, toward the mound.

> GODBOLDT
> Lieutenant, no!

SLOW MOTION: Geoghegan races forward; Godboldt can't stop him, so he charges too. The NVA rocket team is reloading; The Americans on the line shoot down two more NVA running up. As the NVA rocket team fires again, first Geoghegan, and then Godboldt, dive for cover, then Geoghegan runs on. He reaches the mound.

> GEOGHEGAN
> Willie! Grenade!

Godboldt hurls a grenade behind the mound. It wounds the three NVA who are there...

BEHIND THE MOUND, the wounded NVA wait with their AK-47s pointed to either side, ready to shoot Geoghegan no matter which way he comes.

He runs OVER THE TOP of the mound, shooting all three. He races back to the line. Godboldt starts to follow, and gets hit.

> TROOPER
> Godboldt!

> GEOGHEGAN
> I'll get him!

Geoghegan runs back out toward Godboldt...

170   INT. NVA BUNKER - ON THE MOUNTAIN - DAY   170

      Colonel Ahn is watching his maps, getting reports.

                          NVA OFFICER
                    We are through their lines on all sides!
                    Congratulations, Colonel. You have
                    beaten the Americans.

171   AT MOORE'S COMMAND POST   171

      Everything is near chaos.

                          DILLON
                    Colonel, the perimeter is collapsing.
                    Company C is being overrun. A and B
                    can't hold.

      Moore is upright in the gunfire, now raking in waves across
      the clearing and the command post. The din of battle is
      ferocious around him. But as we focus on Moore, the
      SURROUNDING SOUND DIMINISHES from his SUBJECTIVE POV...he
      tunes the noise out in his mind, and looks around at the
      battle... What should he do that he's not doing? What is he
      doing that he shouldn't do?... He turns to his Air
      Controller, CHARLIE HASTINGS.

                          MOORE
                    Hastings--Broken Arrow.

      Everyone in the command unit looks at Moore, and Hastings
      nods and speaks into his field radio.

                          HASTINGS
                    Broken Arrow! Repeat--

172   INT. A SAIGON WAR ROOM   172

      They hear Hastings' voice over their monitors--

                          HASTINGS (ON RADIO)
                    ...Broken Arrow!

      The diplomatic spook looks at the intelligence officer.

                          ARMY INTELLIGENCE OFFICER
                    That means an American unit is being
                    overrun. It calls every combat aircraft
                    in for support.

                          DIPLOMATIC SPOOK
                    My God, there's no hiding it now.

VARIOUS SHOTS - BROKEN ARROW

173   --As the command goes out, carrier flight-crews spring into action; carrier jets take off...   173
174   --fighter-bombers take off from air strips...   174
175   --planes already on missions divert their course, to head for X-Ray...   175
176   --and American generals and diplomats, waiting in Saigon, listen anxiously to reports.   176

177   EXT. HAL MOORE, BY THE TERMITE MOUND - DAY   177

The sound of combat is unbelievable--and all the more desperate now. Shouts over the radio... calls to men who no longer answer...

              MOORE
    C Company! Report!... D Company! Report!...

Nothing comes back.

              HASTINGS
    Planes are on their way, Colonel!

178   AT THE PERIMETERS   178

The NVA sprint in, overrunning a whole company of Americans. They are streaming into the LZ, when...

A fighter-bomber flashes in from overhead and drops two napalm canisters right in the middle of the NVA.

All over the battlefield, all around the surrounded Americans, the planes race in and blast the NVA with napalm and bombs.

179   JOE GALLOWAY   179

is in the medical area, as the doctors go back to helping the wounded. Joe is stunned by the fighting he's just done; dead NVA lie around him. He doesn't know what to do next.

He sees fire slapping into the termite mound near Moore's head (the Command Post is only twenty feet from the medical area). Galloway grabs a fresh magazine of ammo, jams it into the M-16, and fires into the trees where the enemy snipers are. The sniping stops.

Galloway turns and looks at Moore, and Moore is looking back at him; both men realize that Galloway has become not just an observer but a combatant too.

Near Moore, Charlie Hastings, the Air Controller, is shouting into his radio, describing targets... The planes flash in, blowing hell out of everything surrounding them. Hastings turns and shouts to Moore--

                    HASTINGS
     We have planes stacked up every thousand
     feet, from seven to thirty-five thousand!
     We'll get 'em, sir!
          (into radio)
     32-15! 18-7!...

The bombardment is encircling their perimeter with a wall of explosions; but bullets are spatting all around, and Hastings is having trouble handling all the traffic; the planes are coming in fast.

Moore is on another radio, shouting to Crandall--

                    MOORE
     You there, Snake?

180   INTERCUT CRANDALL AND HIS CHOPPERS   180

watching the incredible maelstrom of battle from a mile out. Too Tall, in his chopper, looks over at Crandall; it's hairy.

                    CRANDALL
          (into radio)
     Tell us when, Colonel!

                    MOORE
     Hang back til' there's a lull!

Crandall desperately wants in; he sees the explosions within the ring of battle; his friends are dying; grief and anger wet his eyes, and he pounds his controls in frustration.

                    CRANDALL
     God dammit! God dammit!

181   EXT. LANDING ZONE X-RAY - COMMAND POST - DAY   181

Moore, Plumley and Ouellette take up firing positions on one knee, facing the mountain and the NVA attackers. A tracer hits Ouellette and ricochets off his helmet; As Moore turns to see Ouellette slump over, another movement catches Moore's eye, and he looks up, straight into the noses of two F-100 Super Sabre jet fighters. The lead aircraft releases two shiny, six-foot-long napalm canisters, which slowly begin loblollying end over end toward the Americans.

We see them in SLOW MOTION. They are falling right at Moore, and may wipe out the entire American command center, in the critical moment of battle.

Moore jumps up, waving his arms and screaming at Hastings--

                    MOORE
      Charlie, call that son of a bitch off!
      Call him off!

                    HASTINGS
        (into radio)
      Pull up! Pull up!

The second jet is directly over the command post--its napalm ready to drop right on top of them...but at the last instant it banks off.

The napalm canisters dropped by the first plane slam into the ground and explode, spreading sticky liquid fire over a group of Americans in their little foxholes.

Moore sees his own men dancing in the fire; Plumley, Galloway, and every other American there is horrified, but none so much as Hastings, the Air Controller.

And not only is the napalm burning their own men, but the fire has spread around the ammo dump--all this on top of the enemy attack, with bullets zinging through the command post. As Plumley jumps to beat the fire away from the crates of live ammunition, Moore grabs Hastings, who is so stunned he can't speak or move.

                    MOORE
      Charlie! Listen to me! You're keeping
      us alive! Don't worry about that one.
      Just keep them coming.

Hastings, with trembling hands, lifts his maps and radio.

                    HASTINGS
      Seven-oh-two, attack against the tree
      line, north side of perimeter...

The jets dart in again, with flashing napalm and bombs.

As the flame from the errant napalm cannisters dies down enough, Galloway and several others run to help the burned troopers. Galloway falls to his knees beside a charred man who is screaming in agony. It is Jimmy Nakayama.

AN INSTANT FREEZEFRAME OF JOE'S PHOTOGRAPH

showing NAKAYAMA and his buddies, under fire, but flashing V for Victory signs. Now--

THE PRESENT, AND JOE is horrified, seeing this once smiling face now scorched and mutilated.

                    GALLOWAY
            Medic!

A Medic runs toward them, and is shot in the head.

A medical sergeant runs over and injects Nakayama with morphine.

182   EXT. CRANDALL, IN HIS HELICOPTER - DAY   182

Crandall sees the jets pounding away; he knows how desperate it is down there. He radios Too Tall.

                    CRANDALL
            They can't wait any longer!

                    TOO TALL
            I'm with you, Snake!

Crandall shoves the controls and guns toward the landing zone. His other choppers follow.

183   GALLOWAY AND NAKAYAMA   183

The morphine doesn't help much; Nakayama still cries out in agony. They see Crandall's chopper settling to earth.

                    GALLOWAY
            We've got to get him to the airlift!

Galloway grips Nakayama's charred ankles, and the wounded man SCREAMS; the boots and flesh crumbled in Galloway's hands, and he feels the bones beneath. Stiffening himself to the task, Galloway helps the medic carry Nakayama to the helicopter zone, as bullets buzz through the air like supersonic bees.

They reach the helicopters, and set Nakayama down. The screams, the bullets, the roar of the helicopters...it all crashes around Joe's ears, but he hears none of it...except those screams.

The helicopter crews and the ground troopers are off-loading ammo and making room for the wounded; Galloway sags beside Nakayama.

                        VOICE OVER
              On that same day, as Jimmy Nakayama's
              screams cut the air above the sound of
              battle, his wife was screaming in
              childbirth, half a world away...

184   INTERCUT - A TINY ARMY BASE HOSPITAL IN TEXAS where Jimmy   184
      Nakayama's wife, with a smiling picture of Jimmy on the table
      beside her, gives birth to a baby girl.

                        VOICE OVER (cont'd)
              She gave birth to their daughter, on the
              day Jimmy died.

185   BACK ON THE BATTLEFIELD, JOE GALLOWAY watches Jimmy   185
      Nakayama's charred body being loaded onto a helicopter,
      praying him away into the hands of Crandall, and God.

      The helicopter roars into the gunfire and the sky. It is a
      magnificent picture, but Joe doesn't even think about that.
      And he's lost all sense of danger. He turns slowly and moves
      back to the termite hill.

      He finds his camera, lying beside his rifle. He stares down
      at both.

      He picks up the camera. Reloads it with film...and moves
      off.

186   ON THE CHARLIE COMPANY LINE   186

      They are being overrun, but the airstrikes hit so close, so
      relentlessly, and, along with the resistance of the Americans
      fighting hand to hand, beat back the enemy attack.

      Joe Galloway is there with his camera, and shoots pictures
      instead of bullets; we INTERCUT the POV of his still camera
      with FREEZEFRAMES of the pictures he gets of men fighting
      hand-to-hand.

      Suddenly, the fighting has come to a stop, ending as quickly
      as it started. The enemy dead are stacked two and three deep
      in front of the Americans. Galloway gets pictures of this
      too.

      The Americans stare out, waiting; but no attack comes.

187   MOORE'S COMMAND POST - DAY   187

      Moore looks out, listening to the quiet, feeling the flow of
      the battle. Ouellette moans and stirs; Plumley pulls off his
      helmet and a spent bullet drops out.

                    MOORE
            We've backed 'em off, for just a second.

He grabs the radio.

                    MOORE (cont'd)
            Nadal! Attack now, to save the cut-off
            platoon! Don't stop to neutralize
            resistance, just punch through hard and
            fast and get those men.

188   EXT. THE DRY CREEK BED - DAY   188

    Captain Nadal holds his M-16 at the ready and moves forward,
    with the other Air Cav troopers following.

    They hear the cracks of enemy fire and the bullets slicing
    the air around them; Nadal and several others fire in the
    direction of the enemy but don't stop to flush them out; they
    keep pushing ahead.

    They pick their way through blown-down trees, anthills, and
    scrub brush. They reach the spot where they think the cut-
    off platoon should be, but don't see anybody. Nadal hollers--

                    NADAL
            Are you guys still there?

    Savage sits up, and waves; it's as if the ground has come to
    life; all the artillery has blown dirt and dust over them, so
    they look like part of the earth.

    Nadal and the rest of the relief troops move to the cut-off
    platoon. They find all twenty-nine; nine dead, thirteen
    wounded and heavily bandaged, seven unscratched--all
    incredibly filthy, exhausted, and so parched for water that
    their lips are cracked. And still in shock; seeing Nadal
    standing upright over him, Bungum yells--

                    BUNGUM
            Get down!

                    NADAL
            It's OK, come on, let's go.

    The relief troops hand their canteens to the survivors.
    Nadal notices something on the ground, and picks it up: a
    diary in the hand of a dead NVA soldier. It's delicate,
    quite beautiful, filled with graceful script in Vietnamese.

                    NADAL (cont'd)
            Anybody see any other Vietnamese
            documents?

Nadal's men shake their heads. The sun is going down. They begin taking fire.

                    NADAL (cont'd)
          Let's go.

They pick up the wounded and then the dead. Lieutenant Herrick is the last man they lift. They move out, back toward X-Ray and the American perimeter. Bungum looks at the men helping him walk...

                    BUNGUM
          This ain't over.

189   EXT. HORIZON - SUNSET   189

      Night is falling again on Landing Zone X-Ray.

190   EXT. MOORE'S COMMAND POST - NIGHT   190

The members of the cut-off platoon arrive at the medical area behind the termite mound, and drop to the ground; other troopers carry in the dead. All the stress of the last days starts to flood over Ernie Savage; he's about to break down when he sees Moore standing beside him.

The two men look at each other. There are no words. Moore just nods to Savage in salute, and Savage nods back.

Plumley moves over to Savage.

                    PLUMLEY
          Nice day, Sergeant Savage.

Galloway watches as Crandall and his squad drop off a fresh group of troopers; they look surprisingly clean in contrast to the others, so filthy with battle. Edwards and Arrington, both still alive, are loaded onto Crandall's chopper. Near the med tent a Huey is being packed with a load of dead. Moore watches, as Plumley hands him an accounting.

                    PLUMLEY (cont'd)
          Forty dead. And two unaccounted for.

Galloway moves to Moore.

                    GALLOWAY
          Are these the last of your troopers?

Moore nods. Galloway looks at the Chinook packed with dead.

                    GALLOWAY (cont'd)
                They're going out faster than they're
                coming in.

He's right; the dead outnumber the new arrivals. The
arrivals see it too: as the Hueys lift away, blood seeps off
the edges of the doors. Moore sees his new men are sick and
frightened. He turns to their Captain.

                    MOORE
                Most of Charlie Company was in those
                choppers. I want your men to take their
                place. Come on, I'll show you.

191   INT. NORTH VIETNAMESE BUNKER - NIGHT   191

Colonel Ahn is surrounded by his officers, studying charts,
planning; he steps out of his bunker and sees the moon
rising. For a fleeting moment, he appreciates the beauty.

192   EXT. CHARLIE COMPANY LINES - NIGHT   192

As a bright, near-full moon rises over LZ X-Ray, Moore and
Plumley lead the last arrivals to the position left by the
dead of Charlie Company, where the worst fighting has been.
They climb into the fighting holes. Moore feels something
wet and slick on his fingers, where he touched the wall of
the hole; it's blood. He stares at the space between them
and the mountain, a vista of tall grass and shattered trees,
surreal in the moonlight. Weird, echoing sounds float across
the field. NVA bodies lie dead and stinking just outside the
fighting holes.

                    PLUMLEY
                Better dig in some firing steps. And
                throw some dirt up on those bodies. Keep
                the smell down.

Plumley looks at Moore.

                    PLUMLEY (cont'd)
                Kinda makes you wish you'd signed up for
                submarines, don't it?

The new men are pale, in the new blood and the moonlight. As
they start to dig in, Ouellette moves up with Moore's radio.

                    OUELLETTE
                Colonel, Brigade headquarters wants you
                lifted out on the first chopper at dawn.

                    MOORE
          What idiot would keep ordering that, in
          the middle of a goddamn battle?!

Ouellette covers the receiver lest someone on the other end
might hear Moore's outburst.

                    OUELLETTE
          They said, uh, General Westmoreland wants
          a briefing.

Moore grabs the Headquarters radio.

                    MOORE
               (into radio)
          I am in a fight and object to this order
          to come to Saigon! I WILL NOT LEAVE MY
          MEN, AM I CLEAR?

Moore rings off without waiting for an answer. Out beyond
their line, distant whistles and bugle calls echo eerily down
the mountain. The hopelessness of the situation seems to
ooze up from the dark ground.

                    MOORE (cont'd)
          We have two men unaccounted for. The
          worst fighting was here. They must be
          out there somewhere.

Moore looks out toward the killing ground in front of them.
Haunted, terrifying in the darkness.

                    MOORE (cont'd)
          I'm leading a recon out to find them.

                    PLUMLEY
          I'll go with ya.

193   EXT. IN FRONT OF CHARLIE COMPANY LINES - NIGHT   193

      It's horribly spooky as Moore, Plumley, and four others step
      from the holes, their M-16s ready, and move forward through
      the bodies of the dead NVA. Every corpse looks undead, every
      shadow looks like a sniper, every sound seems like a rifle
      safety being clicked off. Then--

                    PLUMLEY
          Colonel...

      Plumley has found two Americans lying out in the killing
      ground among the NVA bodies--a black soldier and a white one,
      lying entwined.

Plumley lifts the black one, and Moore stoops to pick up the man under him, who fell trying to carry the first soldier to safety. As Moore turns him over and sees who he is, his eyes are stabbed with pain...

194 CLOSE - A FRONT DOOR, AS JULIE KNOCKS   194

Barbara opens the door, to see Julie holding a telegram. The pain on Julie's face silences Barbara.

> JULIE
> They brought... another...
>
> BARBARA
> Oh Julie, Julie...it's yours.
>
> JULIE
> No. It's yours.

195 INT. GEOGHEGAN'S LIVING ROOM - DAY   195

Julie and Barbara sit on the couch, Barbara holding the baby. Maybe it's all the grief they've already experienced that makes Barbara seem so accepting of her news.

> BARBARA
> I thought I had beaten it. I thought we'd seen the last one.
>   (beat)
> Do you want...coffee?
>
> JULIE
> No... Barbara, I...
>
> BARBARA
> You know, I watched everybody react in their own way. I didn't know how it would be with me. Now I still don't.
>
> JULIE
> You're so brave. You're so much braver than me.
>
> BARBARA
> Nobody's braver than you, Julie.
>
> JULIE
> I'm not brave. When that first cab driver came to my house, I was praying that it be a mistake, that it be anybody else but me. And I don't think I'm ever gonna forgive myself for that prayer.

Barbara reaches for Julie and hugs her.

                    JULIE (cont'd)
          You know I told you I'd never seen my
          husband cry. I've realized
          something...he's never seen me cry
          either.

     And now they both let go of all their tears--for themselves,
     for everyone who's lost a husband, a son, a father in war.

196 EXT. LANDING ZONE X-RAY - COMMAND POST - NIGHT   196

     SUPERIMPOSE:

                    4:22 A.M.   The Third Day

     The landing zone seems quiet by comparison--just the distant
     screams from the perimeter and the sporadic snap of sniper
     fire. Beside the medical tent, Colonel Moore holds the
     lifeless body of Jack Geoghegan cradled in his arms, as he
     would hold his own son in the same circumstance. The body of
     Willie Godboldt, the black soldier Geoghegan tried to save,
     is lying next to them, and Moore squeezes Godboldt's dead
     hand. The other soldiers of the Command Post watch
     reverently, as Moore weeps, all the pain washing over him.
     He cradles Geoghegan's body and looks up at Plumley...

                         MOORE
               He died keeping my promise.

                         DILLON
               Sir...they've ordered us out. All of us
               now. They say they'll march
               reinforcements in.

     Moore lays Geoghegan's body softly to earth, and rises. He
     looks around at his battered, depleted command group.

                         MOORE
               They don't understand. We can't get out.

     He looks off toward the mountain, where he knows Colonel Ahn
     is plotting.

                         MOORE (cont'd)
               He's out there, waiting for that. The
               minute he sees helicopters leaving with
               live soldiers, they'll be all over us.
               And he'll have his massacre.

     There's nothing to say. Then Ernie Savage, slumped with the
     rest of the cut-off platoon in the medical area, stands and
     approaches Moore.

                         SAVAGE
               Sir...request permission to rejoin the
               line.

Moore, stirred by Savage's courage, nods; Savage says nothing
to his men, just lifts his weapon and moves off into the
night. The rest of his men, even the wounded, follow him.

Moore stands watching them go. He looks around the
perimeter, sensing, calculating, feeling. Plumley moves up
and stands beside him. Galloway's there too, silent.

                         MOORE
               You ever wonder what went through
               Custer's mind at the moment he realized
               he'd led his men into a slaughter?

                         PLUMLEY
               Sir, Custer was a pussy.

Moore looks at Plumley...his hero.

                         PLUMLEY (cont'd)
               You ain't.

Moore doesn't smile. And then he does. He stares off at the
mountain again. The banshee sounds of bugle and whistle
calls echo down to them.

                         MOORE
               Right now, they're planning the attack
               that'll finish us. They'll keep nibbling
               at us all night, then come at dawn, with
               everything they have. That's what I'd
               do, if I was him.
                    (beat)
               Issue the rest of the ammunition. And
               tell the men to fix their bayonets.

197   EXT. LANDING ZONE X-RAY - OUT ON THE PERIMETER - NIGHT   197

      All along the line, the exhausted troopers receive ammunition
      and the whispered order to fix bayonets.

198   EXT. LANDING ZONE X-RAY - OUTSIDE THE PERIMETER - NIGHT   198

      Beyond the American lines, the North Vietnamese--great masses
      of them--move into position for the final assault. NVA
      snipers are working their way into the trees. It's amazing
      to watch them do it; silently, moving lithe bodies like
      snakes into the upper branches, hidden among the foliage;
      tying themselves into position, readying rifles. And the
      main body of NVA infantry prepares for its charge.

199   EXT. LANDING ZONE X-RAY - FRONT LINE - DAWN   199

   The sky is turning pink, casting a glow over the quiet
   battlefield, covered with the dead.

200   INT. NVA BUNKER - ON THE MOUNTAIN - DAY   200

   Colonel Ahn is coldly sober. He stares at his maps, with his
   forces massed to converge on the weak spot of Charlie
   Company, the exposed place he's attacked all along. A young,
   tough officer, an NVA captain, salutes him and hurries out.

201   EXT. LANDING ZONE X-RAY - CHARLIE COMPANY LINES - DAWN   201

   Moore is at the forward fighting hole. He watches the sun
   crack the horizon with yellow light, and knows this is a
   morning for massacre...

   ON THE NVA LINE, the tough captain looks over his troops,
   deployed for the assault, and lifts his hand to set off the
   final charge... bullets cut into him! Moore and his men are
   charging into them! The NVA are caught by surprise, the
   Americans slamming into them, firing weapons at full auto.
   And every American on the line is firing at the same time,
   high into the trees.

   Snipers in the trees drop from their perches and get caught
   in their rigging. Other NVA, having crawled close to the
   American lines, jump up from the grass and try to run, and
   are cut down.

   THE NORTH VIETNAMESE are not prepared for the sight of the
   screaming Americans running into and through them. The NVA
   have no defenses, no fighting holes dug. Moore and his men,
   cut through them.

   The NVA don't crumble; one of them shouts a warning over his
   radio before he dies.

   Moore leads his men on, changing clips as they run.

   IN THE NVA REAR, men rally to meet the charge; their AKs,
   machine guns, and rocket launchers ready. They see Moore and
   his men coming, and are about to wipe them out when...

   CRANDALL AND HIS HUEYS come ripping by, skimming a few feet
   above the earth, just over the heads of Moore's men and
   firing their M-60 door guns, and gatlings, spewing death.

   MOORE AND HIS MEN run for 500 yards; they reach the base of
   the mountain, and stop.

   There is no more resistance.

202   INT. COLONEL AHN'S UNDERGROUND BUNKER - DAY   202

   Ahn and his aides study his charts, as the NVA Officer rushes
   in.

                        NVA OFFICER
              Colonel! The Americans have broken
              through our lines! We have no soldiers
              between them and our command post!

   Ahn does not panic, but wastes no time. He rolls up his
   charts, and his aides hurriedly do the same, gathering them
   to abandon the command post.

203   EXT. THE KILLING GROUND - DAY   203

   It is a field littered with enemy dead, sprawled in bunches
   across a torn and gouged land; broken bodies, torn uniforms,
   shattered weapons littering the landscape. Galloway moves
   among the dead, taking pictures.

   He comes upon Moore, standing alone, looking over the field,
   tears welling in his eyes. Galloway lifts his camera...then
   lowers it, without taking the picture. Moore moves back
   toward his Command Post.

   Savage and others are policing the battlefield. Savage
   reaches into the grass and picks up something shiny, and
   strange:

   A BUGLE

   A big, battered old army bugle, carrying a French
   manufacturing inscription; it is the bugle taken from the
   French when they were massacred.

   Savage hangs it around his neck, and moves on.

204   EXT. THE MEDICAL AREA - DAY   204

   Crandall is landing, with the rest of his choppers, settling
   in unopposed. Through the glass bubble of his cockpit he
   looks at Moore, and tosses him a salute.

   Moore and Plumley zip up the body bags that contain the
   mortal remains of Jack Geoghegan and Willie Godboldt.

   Captain Dillon approaches Moore.

                    DILLON
          Colonel, we've been checking the enemy
          bodies for documents, and found this on
          the man who tried to bayonet you. I've
          read some of it, it's personal...

Ouellette, at the radio, interrupts...

                    OUELLETTE
          Sir...reinforcements are approaching.

205   EXT. THE RELIEF COLUMN - DAY   205

     A column of fresh American troops is marching overland, led
     by a recon platoon; they enter X-Ray, and the fresh troopers
     are stunned by what they see: bodies of enemy dead, stacked
     like cordwood alongside the trail, in piles six feet high.

     There are also incredible piles of captured enemy weapons and
     gear.

     Nadal meets their wide-eyed leader, LT. COLONEL LIST.

                    LIST
          My God, there's enemy bodies all over
          this valley! For the last thirty minutes
          we've been walking through bodies. What
          happened here?

     Nadal doesn't know how to tell him.

206   EXT. LZ X-RAY - COMMAND POST - DAY   206

     List approaches Moore, and salutes.

                    LIST
          Congratulations on your victory here,
          Colonel Moore.

     Moore looks at List with barely concealed disapproval.

                    MOORE
          We need to step up our harassing
          artillery fire and keep the air strikes
          coming on the slopes.

                    LIST
              (smiling)
          Don't worry, we can handle it.

                    MOORE
          They've retreated, but they're not gone.

> LIST
> We'll take care of it.

> MOORE
> Intelligence marks two other landing zones on our maps. But they can't be defended. Don't go to them.

> LIST
> We've got it, Colonel. You guys better get going! Headquarters is anxious to see you.

207 INT. NVA BUNKER - DAY   207

Colonel Ahn's bunker is deserted, except for Ahn. His men have picked clean every bit of paper, they've stripped the bunker of everything; they're leaving.

Ahn looks back at the empty bunker--with respect. He turns and walks away--but nothing in him is defeated.

208 AT THE LZ - DAY   208

A HUGE CHINOOK HELICOPTER settles down, loaded with reporters, photographers and television crews, under escort of the divisions public-affairs officer.

Joe Galloway, grimy, numb and half-deafened by two days of battle, stands at the landing zone watching his fellow reporters step out and look around, trying to make sense of it all. Spotting Galloway, they move to him, just as artillery rounds scream overhead, impacting on the mountain above them; the flock of reporters flop to the ground.

Galloway stares down at them, realizing the gulf that now exists between him and others of his profession.

> GALLOWAY
> That's friendly artillery.

He walks away.

209 EXT. LANDING ZONE X-RAY - DAY   209

The replacements are walking among the hundreds of enemy dead, picking up huge stacks of weapons, near the spot where Charlie Company made its stand.

Not far from them, the last of the American wounded are climbing onto the Hueys that will ferry them back to hospitals and, ultimately, back to combat.

The wounded pass the bodies of their dead fellow troopers, awaiting the long trip back home.

Near the termite mound that marked the command post, some trooper has shoved a tiny American flag onto a shattered tree trunk; REPORTERS shoot snapshots of it; others cluster around Moore.

                    REPORTER 1
         What was the key to your victory, Colonel?

                    REPORTER 2
         Tell us how you feel.

Moore looks at them. He tries to speak. But he doesn't have the words for the truth. He just walks away.

210   EXT. LZ X-RAY - BY THE HUEY HELICOPTERS - DAY   210

Galloway shoots a few final photos of weary soldiers dragging themselves to the helicopters; emphasized by Galloway's still shots, we see Edwards (wounded), Beck, Savage, Nadal, getting on choppers. Then Galloway picks up his own rifle and pack, to leave. He spots Moore, standing by the helicopters landing to take the dead, and approaches him.

                    GALLOWAY
         Colonel, I just came to say...

But Galloway can't find words either. He looks away, trying not to show the tears welling into his eyes. Moore salutes Galloway. Galloway nods, returns the salute, and moves to a waiting Huey--but he doesn't get on yet.

He sees Moore watching his last three dead--Geoghegan's body being the last--loaded onto a chopper.

Moore looks around the field one last time.

                    VOICE OVER
         The American replacements counted over a thousand NVA bodies.

The reinforcements' Chaplain sets up a small display of Buddhist prayer flags and incense sticks, and then makes the sign of the cross over the bodies.

                    VOICE OVER (cont'd)
         How many more of their comrades were dragged away, or never found, is uncertain. But the Vietnamese believe that if a man is blown apart, then his soul must walk the earth.
                    (MORE)

                    VOICE OVER (cont'd)
          So many were killed by fire and artillery
          that the Vietnamese are afraid to return
          to the place of the battle, and to this
          day it is known as "The Valley of the
          Screaming Souls."

     Galloway gets onto the chopper. Plumley, Hastings and
     Ouellette step on behind him. Galloway looks back as Hal
     Moore, with all of his men, living and dead, already off the
     field, steps onto Crandall's helicopter. We see his boot as
     it lifts off the soil.

211 INT. CRANDALL'S CHOPPER - DAY   211

     Moore looks down at the battle-scarred earth and shattered
     trees. He sees Galloway watching him, and knows Galloway has
     seen the tears welling in his eyes.

                    MOORE
          I'll never forgive myself.

                    GALLOWAY
          For what?

                    MOORE
          That my men died. And I didn't.

     Hal Moore weeps.

212 EXT. CAMP HOLLOWAY - DAY   212

     The big Chinooks settle down. The troopers step off,
     incredibly filthy and exhausted.

     The soldiers of the camp look at these men with something
     approaching awe. Then, with no one giving the order, the Cav
     troopers dress their lines and march off together.

213 EXT. CRANDALL'S LANDING PAD - DAY   213

     Crandall lands. Moore steps out of the helicopter; there is
     no one there to greet him.

     Plumley steps from the chopper, as Crandall and Mills get out
     too.

                    MOORE
          Sergeant Major. Are the wounded--

                    PLUMLEY
          All at the hospital. The Colonel's been
          without sleep for four days. Wouldn't he
          like some rest?

214 BATTERED EARTH - THE GECKO   214

    emerges from his hole and climbs onto a scorched tree.
    Beyond him, LZ X-RAY is battle-scarred and quiet.

215 INT. COMMAND TENT - CAMP HOLLOWAY - DAY   215

    Moore has fallen asleep on a cot; he wakes to find the tent
    full of activity; the radios are crackling, the command tent
    full of concerned men. Moore sees Plumley and Dillon among
    them.

                        MOORE
              What's going on?

                        PLUMLEY
              Apparently...the replacement battalion
              was ambushed, moving to the new landing
              zone.

                        MOORE
              Ambushed?! How--

                        PLUMLEY
              Apparently, while they were marching they
              got strung out and--

                        MOORE
              Marching?!

    Nobody wants to look Moore in the eye. They hear the radio
    voices from the fighting, confused, terrified...

                        RADIO VOICES
              Where are they?! Where-- what--

                        MOORE
              They're panicking! What's their
              commander doing?

                        DILLON
              He has all his officers up at the front
              of the column...

                        MOORE
              He just came off a desk job! Somebody's
              got to go in and pull them out!

    Moore grabs his rifle and his gear. He's running for the
    door when he collides with Colonel Brown, entering.

                        COLONEL BROWN
            We've ordered Diduryk's company to saddle
            up. General Westmoreland's sent for you.
            The Secretary of Defense is in Saigon and
            wants you to brief him on your battle.

    The radios still crackle with the chaos of the unfolding
    massacre--and Moore has the terrible realization that his
    superiors aren't going to let him go back out.

216 INT. U.S. ARMY HEADQUARTERS - SAIGON - HALLWAY - DAY   216

    Hal Moore stands straight up, in his battle fatigues, in a
    Colonial hallway. GENERAL WESTMORELAND steps out and gives
    him a huge smile and a handshake and ushers him into

217 INT. U.S. ARMY HEADQUARTERS - SAIGON - FORMAL OFFICE - DAY   217

    ROBERT McNAMARA and several Generals and Washington aides are
    there.

                        GENERAL WESTMORELAND
            Mr. Secretary, this is Colonel Moore.
            Colonel Moore, the Secretary of Defense.

    McNamara is beaming, and shakes Moore's hand warmly.

                        MCNAMARA
            Colonel, you have the thanks of your
            whole country--especially mine, and that
            of the President. You've won a victory
            that's inspired us all. And made us sure
            of our ultimate victory.

                        MOORE
            My men...are the finest who ever wore the
            uniform.

                        MCNAMARA
            We know that! And they dismembered the
            enemy. 79 dead, against 1800 to 2000
            enemy? That's in the range of 22.8 to
            26.2 to one!

    For a moment, Moore can't get a word out. He reaches into a
    pocket and withdraws the small, beautiful book Nadal found
    beside the cut-off platoon.

                        MOORE
            One of my men...found this on the
            battlefield. Vietnamese. I had it
            translated.
                (he reads)
                        (MORE)

                    MOORE (cont'd)
          "Oh, my dear, my young wife. When the
          troops come home after the victory, and
          you do not see me, please look at the
          proud colors. You will see me there, and
          you will feel warm under the shadow of
          the bamboo tree."

The General and the Diplomat don't understand; they smile, thinking Moore is understandably befuddled.

                    GENERAL WESTMORELAND
          We're requesting 40,000 more troops, and
          because of what your men have proven, we
          expect the President to look very
          favorably on our request. We'll run
          these little bastards back home.

Moore struggles to find the words.

                    MOORE
          I just...I want you all to
          understand...how well my men fought. How
          proud of them I am.

                    MCNAMARA
          Yes, yes, of course we do--

                    MOORE
          But if I were the leader of the other
          side...I would have been proud of them.

Dead silence; they're not sure what Moore is trying to say, or if they want to hear it.

                    MOORE (cont'd)
          They pushed 2000 men through artillery
          and napalm. And those 2000 came
          willingly. They ran right at the muzzles
          of our guns. We took them hand to hand.
          And we won. But they didn't see it that
          way. They didn't go away. They just
          backed up and came again.
               (beat)
          We won't run the little bastards home,
          Sir. They are home.

McNamara is no longer smiling, nor is anyone else.

On Moore, as he looks at them...we DISSOLVE TO:

218   EXT. LZ X-RAY - DUSK   218

It looks empty, except for the dead North Vietnamese.

But as we PAN we see NVA soldiers appearing like ghosts congealing out of the twilight, silently picking up their fallen comrades.

And at the termite hill, where Moore had his command post, is Colonel Ahn.

Ahn looks around from the perspective Moore had, projecting himself into his enemy's mind. Ahn sees the dead bodies of his men, so close by; the bullet marks in the termite mound; the American blood on the ground, where the wounded and dying lay. Ahn says to one of his staff officers--

> AHN
> He was brilliant. As smart as he was brave. They all were.

He notices the tiny American flag, stuck into the shattered tree trunk. Ahn admires it, but shakes his head sadly.

> AHN (cont'd)
> Such a tragedy. They will think this was their victory. So this will become an American war. And the end will be the same, except for the numbers who die before we get there.

His soldiers, carrying their fallen brothers, melt back into the mists and vegetation, as does Colonel Ahn. In but a moment, it's as if they were never there.

219 EXT. MOORE'S HOUSE - NIGHT   219

The windows are lit against the damp night. The street outside is empty as a graveyard.

220 INT. MOORE'S HOUSE - NIGHT   220

The boys are making playful noises upstairs. Julie sits with her DAUGHTERS, the eldest reading "The Little Star" to Cecile...

> ELDER DAUGHTER
> "... and that was the most beautiful night since the creation of the earth."

> JULIE
> Okay, brush your teeth.

> ELDER DAUGHTER
> Aw, Mom--

                    JULIE
          No whining, let's go!

The girls head upstairs.

OUTSIDE, A CAB slides to a silent stop on the street.

INSIDE, Julie picks up a ripped pair of jeans and starts repairing the knees. There is a KNOCK at the door. And it's too late for visitors. Julie looks outside and sees the cab there. Her heart stops.

                    JULIE
              (calling upstairs)
          Kids... get in bed.

                    KIDS
              (from upstairs)
          Mom...

                    JULIE
          Get in bed!

Another soft knock. She moves to the door. She can't look. She opens the door.

It's Hal.

He moves in and takes her into his arms.

The kids are peeking from the top of the stairs. Julie's face is still buried in Hal's chest. Then she says the words she has prayed to say --

                    JULIE (cont'd)
          Children!... Your daddy's home.

221   INT. AIRPORT - DAY   221

Bill Beck helps Russell Adams from the plane. Adams is in a wheelchair, his head bandaged, half his brain blow away. No one at the airport pays them any attention at all, as they move down a long corridor, alone.

                    MOORE'S VOICE OVER
          Some had families waiting. For others,
          their only family would be the men they
          had bled beside. There were no bands, no
          flags, no honor guards to welcome them
          home. They went to war because their
          country ordered them to. But in the end
          they fought not for their country, or
          their flag. They fought for each other.

222 JOE GALLOWAY is in a newsroom back in America; all around him journalists are writing about sports, politics, society; life seems normal to them. Joe's eyes are haunted as he types...

We see images of the young men fighting and dying at X-Ray. Men like Beck and Adams, as Adams takes a bullet in the head and Beck picks up his machine gun to fight on.

223 INT. BARBARA GEOGHEGAN'S NEW HOUSE - DAY

Barbara sits at her kitchen table, reading a letter from Hal Moore, a letter that brings tears to her eyes. She lowers the letter and inverts the envelope; from it falls the baby bracelet Jack wore when he lived, and died.

224 INT. HANOI HOUSE - DAY

The wife of the soldier who charged Moore with a bayonet, 8 years older than in the photograph we saw of her, sits at a table in her home. In the corner nook is a Buddhist memorial shrine featuring a picture of her husband. She too has received a packet from Hal Moore, wrapped in brown mailing paper. She opens it to find a letter, and the crimson book Lum carried with her picture.

225 HAL MOORE, WALKING ALONE...

It's years later, but he looks very much the same: graying hair, yet his face is still chiseled, his body still lean and tough. He's in civilian clothes now. It's another cold, gray day, and he is

EXT. WASHINGTON, D.C. - AT THE WALL - DAY

Moore walks along the wall, past thousands of names cut into the stone of the memorial. And played out upon the wall, as if projected there from Moore's soul, are his memories: Moore standing in the middle of LZ X-Ray with bullets cutting the air as he waves and screams to ward off the jets dropping napalm; the canisters falling on his men, engulfing them in fire; and Joe Galloway struggling away from the flames, holding the charred legs of Jimmy Nakayama...

> MOORE'S VOICE OVER
> I wish I could find words that would keep war from ever happening again. We who have seen it will never stop seeing. In the silence of the night, we will always hear the screams...

He moves up to the joint of the V, the center of The Wall, where the names of those killed earliest in the war are inscribed. On Panel 3-East he sees the names of his men. His face reflects in the polished granite, as if their names are chiseled on his face.

> MOORE'S VOICE OVER (cont'd)
> But I would not choose to stop. For I would not be without those men, even if all I have left of them is the memory of their sacrifice...

In his memory, projected on the wall across their names, are more flashbacks: Tom Metsker giving up his place on the helicopter to The wounded Captain, and being shot dead as he does so...

226 And then we see the last moments of Jack Geoghegan, fighting in Charlie Company's most desperate moments. Willie Godboldt goes down, out ahead of all the others, and Geoghegan charges forward to save him. He lifts Godboldt, starts back toward the American lines, and is ripped by bullets, going down... 226

> MOORE'S VOICE OVER (cont'd)
> ...For it is the memory of them. And I would not wish to live in a world without such men as these.

227 The images slowly disappear, absorbing into the wall, leaving Hal Moore's face reflected on the polished black stone that bears so many names, as we FADE OUT... 227

Before the final credits, crawling up the screen are the names of the men killed at X-Ray and Albany. All of them.

<u>THE END</u>

SCREENPLAY NOTES AND CHANGES

Movie-making *is an experience of experiment and discovery. Driven by emotion, steered by thought, guided by instinct, the adventure unfolds, complete with twists, turns, dead-ends, disappointments, and unexpected treasures. Nowhere is this more evident than in the writing process; the screenplay can—and should—be the arena of fluid dreaming. The following are notes made by the editors of this publication, filmmakers themselves, based on comparisons of the early drafts of the screenplay with its final product. I asked them simply to point out whatever struck them as interesting as they made these comparisons, in hopes that their observations might prove helpful to other students of the screenwriting craft.*

❖ Following is the original opening scene from an early draft of *We Were Soldiers*.

```
FADE IN:

DARKNESS OF NIGHT

On the horizon, the sun has moved to just below the rim
of the earth, and is beginning to turn the sky purple,
above a hot, dry plain.

In the rising light, we begin to pick up details,
scattered across the earth:  a bare foot here, a ripped
boot there, a torn uniform drenched in blood upon a
mutilated corpse...

More light -- more corpses.  The entire field is strewn
with the bodies of soldiers.  As the SUN CRACKS THE
HORIZON we realize that what we are seeing is the first
dawn after a

MASSACRE
```

Strewn everywhere, fallen in the long dry grass, are what used to be a whole regiment of soldiers. Broken rifles and ruined equipment are sprinkled among the punctured bodies. Trampled into the grass we see a battered BUGLE tied with a torn and bloody banner, telling us that this used to be the U.S. 7th CAVALRY. And we see dead horses, full of arrows; corpses still clutching the broken spears that took young lives... the remnants of CUSTER'S LAST STAND...

But now we hear A NOISE, RISING...a sound that does not belong to the time of horses and arrows; it is a hacking, throbbing, mechanical sound...

THE SUN is a huge red ball at the horizon...and racing in from it, with a DEAFENING ROAR, are...

EIGHT ASSAULT HELICOPTERS

They flare expertly to a hover, and settle suddenly onto the grass. On the nose of the lead helicopter we see a painted yellow banner like the one we saw earlier, trampled to the ground, and it too tells us that this is the U.S. 7th CAVALRY--the Air Cav.

Leaping to the ground is a lean, blond Kentuckian, LT. COLONEL HAROLD "HAL" MOORE. A body like a whip, a man with a thousand-yard stare. What you notice instantly are his eyes. They are not fierce--not exactly--but they are frightening because they have come to find and kill any enemy that will stand before him, and they are not afraid. But they are burning, intense, instantly taking in details, the brain behind them honed to a razor edge by the thousand thoughts racing across it, especially now...

Thirty more soldiers, the first of Moore's regiment, jump from the helicopters behind him. They follow Hal Moore as he leads them in a screaming charge, firing their M-16's on full auto--toward the line of trees encircling their clearing. Behind them, the eight choppers lift off as suddenly as they arrived, and roar away.

Moore and his men reach the trees, and stop firing. The silence is sudden. The helicopters are gone. The woods--a thin stand of trees around the hot, dry grass--seem empty.

THE SILENCE is ominous.

Moore looks around and snaps an order.

>   MOORE
>   Hold and search.

Instantly his men are obeying; they are well trained, and at a high degree of readiness on this, their first combat mission. As half his men form a tight perimeter, their rifles bristling out in a small ring, the others fan out into the grass and the brush, making a quick scout of their surroundings. Moore's eyes scan everything; OVER THIS, we hear his voice, recalling this moment...

>   MOORE (V.O.) (CONT'D)
>   I want you to understand the
>   situation. It was the first assault
>   of the U.S. 7th Cavalry since the
>   Battle of the Little Big Horn. And
>   I was gonna make damn sure that the
>   same thing that had happened to
>   Custer and his men was not gonna
>   happen to Hal Moore, and to mine.

❖ This scene originally preceded Scene 14 in which the Moores arrive in Ft. Benning, GA.

```
INT. MILITARY BASE HOUSING - DAY

The family housing of a military base in 1964 makes a
Motel 6 looks palatial.  And this particular apartment
looks even more crowded because a family of seven live
in it:  five -- count 'em, five -- children, between
the ages of one and ten.

Hal bursts through the front door and pops into the
chaos of the living room.

                    MOORE
          Julie?...Julie!

CECILE, his five-year-old daughter, looks up from her
doll.

                    CECILE
          Hi, Daddy!

                    MOORE
          Hi, honey, where's mom?  Julie?!

He scoops up Cecile and moves toward the kitchen.  As
he does, his eight-year-old son dives at him from the
back of a chair, and Hal catches the boy and swings him
onto his back.  His oldest son, the ten-year-old, grabs
at Hal's legs and pretends to try to tackle him, and
Hal, laughing, drags them all toward

THE KITCHEN

Julie Moore, Hal's wife, is holding her recent baby and
sterilizing baby bottles and rubber nipples by boiling
them on the stove.  Julie is a beautiful woman, even
more beautiful with a baby in her arms.
```

                        HAL
            Julie! I just got word from Harry
            Kinnard!

The water boils over on the stove and Julie spins
quickly to turn down the flame. The baby squeals and
Hal shifts Cecile into one arm and takes the baby with
the other.

                        HAL
            You know that new unit he's
            starting?

                        JULIE
            The air mobility thing?

                        HAL
            They're calling it the Air Cavalry
            now!

Hal is grinning. Air Cavalry! He loves it.

                        JULIE
            And he's giving you a command.

                        HAL
            I'm going to help formulate and
            define the old project! The orders
            just came through. We're going to
            Fort Benning.

                        JULIE
            Georgia?

                        HAL
            They've got better housing than
            here.

Another daughter is crying at Julie's feet; she scoops the girl up. Suddenly Hal and Julie realize they are standing there in a noisy kitchen with their arms full of children; and try as she might, Julie has a troubled look in her eyes. Hal wants to reassure her.

                     HAL
It's just a training assignment.

                    JULIE
This Air Cavalry...where do they mean to use it?

                     HAL
It's a jungle terrain concept.

                    JULIE
That place on the news...? Vietnam.

                     HAL
That's just advisors in a local dispute.

                    JULIE
Like Korea?

With a child in each arm and one on his back, and Julie with one in her arms and one gripping her leg, Hal looks across at his wife.

❖ **Sc. 48:** Originally, this party scene was a private daytime meeting between Moore and General Kinnard at the General's mansion in Kinnard's office. Later, while on set, the scene was changed again. On the following page is the script as marked up by Randall Wallace just prior to shooting.

EXT. COMMANDING GENERAL'S MANSION - FT. BENNING - NIGHT

The officers--about 20 of them--are in their dress uniforms, and their wives are in their prettiest dresses, all gathered under a party tent beneath the oaks of the grounds outside the antebellum residence of the Commanding General. The men are beaming, smoking cigars; Julie is beautiful on Hal's arm, ~~shaking hands, accepting congratulations. General Kinnard moves up to Hal~~ as Hal ~~introduces her~~ she and Hal meet General Kinnard.

GENERAL KINNARD
Hal, can I see you a minute?

He leads Hal to a quieter place, under a tree.

MOORE
And you know my wife, Julie.

GENERAL K
You look so lovely tonight, ~~Mrs~~ Julie.

JULIE
Thank you, General. You're so kind to open your home to us.

GENERAL KINNARD (cont'd)
~~Congratulations, Hal.~~ This deployment's quite a tribute to what you've accomplished in such a short time.

MOORE
Thank you sir. But I didn't hear the President mention a State Of Emergency.

Why the long face?

GENERAL KINNARD
I like to see my boys having fun.

At the bandstand, Crandall jumps on stage, consults with the band leader, and launches into a song. The men ~~and women~~ ~~James is~~ General Kinnard smiles, but sees Hal lost in thought.

G.K.
No, he didn't.

MOORE
And

GENERAL KINNARD
~~That's why I wanted to talk with you.~~ Without that declaration, the enlistments will not be extended. ~~I'm sorry, Hal.~~

GK
I'm sorry, Hal.

MOORE
Forgive me, Sir, but let me get this straight. We form a division using techniques that have never been attempted in battle--against an enemy with twenty years of combat experience, on their ground, twelve thousand miles from our ground. And just before the Army sends us into the fight, they take away a third of my men. The most experienced third, including officers.

~~The small band of Army musicians strikes up Auld Lang Syne. Officers and wives turn tenderly to each other.~~

MOORE
You saw this coming. That's why you sent me that new crop of platoon leaders.

Moore struggles to contain his anger, and face the facts.

MOORE (CONT'D)
Korea didn't teach 'em anything.

GENERAL KINNARD
Politicians?

Crandall ~~waves the stage~~ and the band shifts to a tender love song.

Under the tent, Julie is left alone as other couples cuddle. Hal sees this and starts toward her, but Kinnard stops him one more time.

GENERAL KINNARD
By the way, Hal. Since we're being deployed, they're renumbering the units. You're now the commander of the 1st Battalion of the 7th Cavalry.

MOORE
The 7th? The same regiment as...Custer?

Kinnard nods soberly. Moore nods and moves toward Julie. But she sees something in his eyes as he moves toward her from beneath the oaks, their limbs trailing Spanish moss like the ghosts of hanged men.

❖ This scene from an early draft originally preceded Scene 50 in which Julie visits Barbara to help her prepare for Jack's departure.

```
INT. HOUSE - DAY

Julie is leading the ladies in a class of books.

                    JULIE
          This novel is a great one.  It's about--

Then they all stop; Hal has appeared at the door.  And
all the ladies know what that means.

                    JULIE (CONT'D)
          Hi, Hon.

                    HAL
          Ladies... I've given the men the
          afternoon off.  We'll assemble this
          evening, on the parade ground.

                    ONE OF THE WOMEN
          Does this mean our meetings are
          cancelled?

                    JULIE
          No.  We'll meet tomorrow, just like
          we always do.  But we'll cancel this
          meeting now.  Go home and be with
          your husbands.

The ladies all stand and leave.  But on their way out,
they look at Moore.  The last one is pregnant.

                    PREGNANT WOMAN
          Take care of my husband, Colonel Moore.

                    MOORE
          I will, Rosaria.
```

She leaves, and Hal and Julie are left alone for a long silence.

                JULIE
The two little ones won't know. And John'll be okay about it, I think he'll think it's exciting. Celia and Mark... they're the ones I worry about.

                MOORE
I'll tell them at dinner tonight. We'll try to make it casual.

                JULIE
What time do you leave?

                MOORE
Four tomorrow morning. I'll have to be up at 1:30 to be ready.
                (beat)
So I'll get to tuck them in, that last time...for awhile.

                JULIE
Yeah. For awhile.

                MOORE
I love what you've done for the wives. You don't know how much it means to them.

                JULIE
I know they appreciate it. We've all gotten close.

                MOORE
I mean the men, how much they appreciate it.

>   MOORE (CONT'D)
> The men don't talk about it much, but
> nothing works on a man's mind more
> than worrying about his wife and
> family--and nothing helps like
> knowing they're being looked after...
> 'Cause there's nothing that matters
> more than...

She touches his lips.

>   JULIE
> I know.

>   MOORE
> Julie, I... Just let me say this, the
> best I can. I'm leaving my family
> behind to go lead men into battle.
> It's hard to make sense of it.

>   JULIE
> It's who you are, Hal. It's your
> career, but it's who you are.

>   MOORE
> It's not just that, Julie. I'm a
> soldier, it's true, and I've trained
> my whole life for times like this.
> But I don't love it more than you.
> It's just that-- those men, every
> one of 'em is somebody's son, some
> woman's husband, or gonna be, some
> kid's father. And they're going
> into battle. There's nothing I can
> do to change that. And if they're
> not led right, they'll die. Some of
> 'em may die anyway, but more will
> die if they're led wrong.

                    MOORE (CONT'D)
          I've been in battle and I came home
          to you and my children because God
          and some good officers looked after
          me. And I've got to do the same for
          those men. And someday, when there's
          another war, our sons may be in
          battle, and I want them looked after
          by some officer that will lead them
          right, and put their lives ahead of
          his own. That's what I have to do.

                         JULIE
          Are you gonna say this to me every
          time you go off to fight? If you
          are, maybe we can just write it down
          and have me read it.

He smiles and hugs her.

❖ The following scenes originally preceded Scene 60 in which the American soldiers arrive in Vietnam.

MONTAGE, THE MEN LEAVING: We see Barbara sitting at home, nursing her baby and trying not cry; we see Metsker telling his wife goodbye, and Alma Givens kissing her husband...

                    VOICE OVER
          On the same day the 7th Air Cavalry left
          Charleston Harbor, bound for Vietnam...

EXT. HO CHI MINH TRAIL - DAY

We see North Vietnamese trucks loaded with military supplies being off-loaded onto bicycles, the perfect conveyance for the jungle trails. It's a brilliant adaptation as the army marches south; at the lead is Colonel Ahn.

                    VOICE OVER
          ...the 66th North Vietnamese
          Regiment departed its home in the
          North, to move through its Cambodian
          sanctuary to the Central Highlands
          of South Vietnam.

EXT. NORTH VIETNAMESE BUNKER - NIGHT

Soldiers pushing bicycles move into a cave ramp
concealed with vegetation. As the last man enters its
camouflaged cover shuts; it's as if nothing was ever
there. We PAN the jungle and push down toward the
earth, where...

INT. NORTH VIETNAMESE BUNKER - NIGHT

Colonel Ahn has gathered his officers in an UNDERGROUND
COMMAND BUNKER, carved from the earth, impressively
organized. They are looking at a spy's blown up
black-and-white snapshots of the arrival of the Air Cav
in Vietnam: helicopters, stacks of equipment, and
extremely young men. Ahn speaks with his officers in
VIETNAMESE, WITH SUBTITLES...

                    COLONEL AHN
          These helicopters...the Americans
          call these troops Air Cavalry.

Colonel Ahn looks around at his officers,
battle-hardened veterans.

                    COLONEL AHN (cont'd)
          We must fight these Air Cavalry
          soldiers right away. If we can draw
          them into battle, and annihilate
          every one of them, this war could be
          over.

COLONEL AHN (cont'd)
But to fight the tiger, we must
first lure him from his mountain.

He points to a spot on his maps-- large and detailed.

COLONEL AHN (cont'd)
The American Special Forces Camp at
Plei Me. We attack it, then pull
back and wait for them to come after
us.

NVA OFFICER
How do you know they will come?

COLONEL AHN
They are Americans.

EXT. U.S. SPECIAL FORCES CAMP - PLEI ME - NIGHT

Three GREEN BERETS walk from the mess tent after dinner, relaxed, comfortable...until a bullet slaps one of them in the chest, and mortar rounds fall within their perimeter. In a moment the whole camp is alive, the Green Berets reacting quickly; the two check their friend, see he's dead, and race to the lookout posts along their barbed wire, where sentries are already lighting up the night. But they see no targets.

GREEN BERET
Cease fire!

They scan the brush; nothing. Except a few dead Americans.

GREEN BERET (CONT'D)
Bastards.

❖ The following scenes originally preceded Scene 63, in which the men board the choppers and depart for the battle. This sequence also includes the original introduction of Joe Galloway. The latter scene includes a character named Ladner who was cut from the final shooting script, and more dialogue between Beck and Adams, who fought side by side as an M-60 gunner team.

```
EXT. A TEA PLANTATION - DAY

Galloway flies in and lands.  He joins the Air Cav in
their walk.

                    GALLOWAY
          Hey, soldier, where you guys going?

                    SOLDIER
          We're tracking down infiltrators.

Galloway settles in, walking beside them.  His pack is
just as heavy, he just carries a camera instead of a
gun.  As Galloway marches on, one of the soldiers
whispers to another...

                    SOLDIER (CONT'D)
          He'll quit by noon.

NOON

And Galloway is still marching along, while the
soldiers are dying from the heat.

At sundown they slog through a stream; they get cold
and wet.

EXT. PERIMETER - CAMP HOLLOWAY - NIGHT

Beck, Adams, and Ladner are guarding the perimeter from
a pit; it's quiet, Ladner looking into the darkness as
Beck and Adams mess with cans of water.
```

JOE GALLOWAY, a 23-year-old journalist, cameras hanging around his neck, slides into the fighting hole and startles them.

> GALLOWAY
> Whoa, guys! I'm Joe Galloway.

> ADAMS
> Photographer?

> GALLOWAY
> Reporter. Bureau Chief, U.P.I.

> ADAMS
> That's Beck, he's Ladner, I'm Adams.

Galloway scans the spooky darkness beyond the hole.

> GALLOWAY
> Any action?

> ADAMS
> Yeah. We're makin' coffee.

Adams gives Galloway a metal water cup and Beck hands him a pinch of white clay.

> GALLOWAY
> What's this?

> ADAMS
> C-4. Light it just right, it'll heat a whole can of water.

> GALLOWAY
> What if you light it wrong?

                    BECK
          It blows your arm off.

Galloway's hands are trembling as he touches his
lighter to the C-4; the troopers watch as it flares
suddenly, and they laugh; then they're startled again
as Moore and Plumley slide into the hole. The troopers
salute; Plumley's pissed off.

                    PLUMLEY
          Why weren't we challenged?

                    LADNER
          Sir, we--

                    MOORE
          Who're you?

                    GALLOWAY
          Galloway, Colonel, I'm Bureau Chief
          of-

                    MOORE
          That hot water?

                    GALLOWAY
          Sir? Yes sir, I--

                    MOORE
          Shave with it.

                    GALLOWAY
          Sir?...

                    MOORE
          Everybody shaves in my outfit, boy.
          Even journalists.

                    MOORE (CONT'D)
                    (to his troopers)
          And you. Keep alert. Nothing's
          wrong tonight. Except that
          nothing's wrong.

He and Plumley are about to climb out of the hole when
mortar rounds CRASH within their perimeter. Hell
breaks loose all along the line, the green soldiers
shoot into the night as enemy rounds explode around
them. Moore grabs the radio; he's shockingly cool.

                    MOORE (CONT'D)
                    (into radio)
          This is Moore, we have sappers,
          direct fire at fifty yards and walk
          it out...

Ladner is firing wildly; Beck and Adams are scrambling
for their weapons, but Plumley grabs Ladner's shoulder.

                    PLUMLEY
          What the hell you shootin' at?

Ladner doesn't have a target; he tries to say so, but
no words come out.

                    PLUMLEY (CONT'D)
          Then quit shootin'.

A flaming arc cuts through the air and falls among a
stack of sandbagged crates behind them. Beck sees
this, in sheer terror--

                    BECK
          It's in a grenade box! The whole
          ammo dump's gonna blow!!

The troopers duck, trying to shield themselves against being vaporized. Plumley's disgusted.

> PLUMLEY
> Shit...

He climbs from the hole and moves to the flame spewing shell in the grenade box, as Moore remains on the radio, quietly giving orders. The troopers and Galloway watch wide-eyed as Plumley reaches into the box bare-handed and slings the flare out of the grenades like he'd rid his tent of a dead rat. It sputters out, harmless.

The shooting stops as suddenly as it began. Moore finishes his orders over the radio.

> MOORE
> Secure the perimeter and see to the wounded.

Adams, Beck and Ladner are stunned by the first crack of action, and Moore's shocking coolness as he hands back the radio, then looks at Galloway, whose hands are shaking so badly he's sloshing the water from the can he still holds.

> MOORE (CONT'D)
> And get that shave.

Moore climbs out and walks away with Plumley.

❖ The following scenes originally preceded Scene 123 in which the cut-off platoon clings to its territory. This illustrates the first attempt at the cut-off platoon rescue by one of Nadal's men, Medal of Honor recipient Joe Marm, whose story was omitted from the final shooting script.

EXT. BETWEEN THE CREEK BED AND CUT-OFF PLATOON - DAY

Immediately Marm's men run into heavy enemy fire; fifteen men go down. Marm's medic, Calvin Bouknight, crawls under fire, putting himself between the enemy and a wounded white soldier who is aspirating blood; Bouknight gives the soldier mouth to mouth, then is hit with a buzz bomb that blows a hole in his back; he falls dead, over the man he was helping.

Marm runs to Bouknight and drags his body back, as other troopers get to the wounded and dead and drag them back to the shelter of the creek bed.

EXT. THE CUT-OFF PLATOON, ON THE KNOLL - DAY

Doc Charlie Lose is crawling toward another wounded man when he is shot in the leg.

                   SAVAGE
  Charlie!

But Lose keeps crawling; when he reaches the wounded man, he gives him a toilet paper bandage, then makes a compress for his own leg.

Suddenly the NVA try another mass assault from three directions.

                 SAVAGE (cont'd)
  Full auto!

They put their M-16's on full automatic and kill most of the attacking NVA. One NVA breaks through and is right on top of Savage's back when Lose rolls over with a rifle and shoots him down. The NVA retreat again. When Savage looks at Lose, he sees him bandaging himself again, a new wound in his left arm.

> SAVAGE (cont'd)
> We better burn the codes.

They collect maps, notebooks, and signal operating instructions booklets from the dead commanders and Savage burns them all, as he and his small band hunker down, determined to hold their ground to the end.

❖ **The following scene is another true battlefield story that was omitted from the final shooting script.**

OUT AMONG THE TREES

Plumley runs on, and we stay with VINCENT CANTU, a draftee, hugging the ground as artillery bombards the ground in front of him and bullets cut the air all around him. He glances up and squints; he sees a soldier moving up with cameras dangling around his neck.

Cantu looks, frowns, squints again... He sprints across the corner of the open LZ and dives under a bush where the reporter, Galloway, is kneeling.

> CANTU
> Joe? Joe Galloway? Hey, Joe, don't you remember me?

> VOICE OVER
> In one of those bizarre coincidences of war, two men from a high school class of thirty ran into each other on the battlefield...

> GALLOWAY
> Vince?

                    CANTU
          Vince Cantu, from Refugio High
          School! Hey, Joe, how ya doin',
          man? This here is some bad shit.
          How's things back home?

As the bullets fly around them, and thunk into the tree
that shelters them, they chat about home.

                    GALLOWAY
          Pretty good, they got a stop light.

                    CANTU
          They still got my car for sale at
          the gas station?

                    GALLOWAY
          Willie bought it.

                    CANTU
          Zit-face Willie?

                    GALLOWAY
          Naw, Bow-legged Willie.

                    CANTU
          Bow-legged Willie?! How the hell is
          he?

Cantu ducks around the tree and fires a burst from his
M-16, but remains cheerful; the happiness of seeing an
old friend has swung his mind away from the terror.

                    GALLOWAY
          Pretty good, Vince.

A trooper goes down nearby, and calls--

>   TROOPER
> I'm hit! Medic!

There's no medic around.

>   GALLOWAY
> I got him! Hey, see you later,
> Vince.

>   CANTU
> Sure, Joe!

As Galloway crawls to the wounded trooper to drag him back to the aid station, Cantu calls happily to the troopers fighting beside him.

>   CANTU (cont'd)
> That's Joe Galloway, from my high
> school, man!
>   (fires a burst)
> That Joe, he's a crazy
> motherfucker!...

❖ The following scene originally preceded Scene 190 in which the cut-off platoon returns to Moore's Command Post.

AT THE COMMAND POST

They realize the sound of battle is dying down all around them. A spooky calm descends on the field.

The men in the Command Post look at each other, and then at Moore. Is it over? Moore doesn't think so.

>   MOORE
> I want four companies to advance 300
> yards. Recover any wounded--or
> dead.

ALL AROUND - VARIOUS SHOTS

Moore's men, filthy and tired, move forward on the field. They receive only sporadic fire, and fire back as necessary.

THE BATTLEFIELD

is a haunting place of heroism and loss... Bill Beck finds a dead trooper locked in contact with a dead NVA, the American's hands around the NVA's throat; other troopers find two Cav troopers linked together, one Black and one Hispanic, having died trying to drag each other back to the lines.

Moore's men begin to retrieve the bodies of their comrades.

❖ Following is a sequence that expanded Scenes 192 and 193, in which Moore leads the recon mission to find the two unaccounted for soldiers. This handwritten original version was written by Randall Wallace on the back of his script.

The hopelessness of the situation seems to ooze up from the dark ground.

MOORE
We have two men unaccounted for. The worst fighting was here. They must be out there somewhere.

Moore looks out toward the killing ground in front of them. ~~Nobody want to go out there~~ Haunted, terrifying in the darkness.

> MOORE
> I'm leading a recon out to find them.
>
> PLUMLEY
> I'll go with you.
>
> EXT. IN FRONT OF CHARLIE COMPANY LINES - NIGHT
>
> It's horribly spooky as Moore, Plumley, and for others step from the holes and move forward, through the bodies of the dead NVA. Every corpse looks ~~untold~~ undead, every shadow looks like a sniper, every sound seems like a rifle safety being clicked off.
>
> Their M-16's ready, they move through the dark killing ground. Then —

❖ The following scene originally preceded Scene 196 in which the cut-off platoon soldier Savage requests permission to rejoin the line.

HAL MOORE, curled up in his poncho on the bare ground beneath the stars; he's trying to grab a few minutes of sleep, but it won't come.

He slips off the poncho, and moves up to Plumley, who can't sleep either.

>   MOORE
>   It's not over.
>
>   PLUMLEY
>   Naw, sir, it ain't.
>
>   MOORE
>   The next day...it'll be the worst of
>   all. These NVR's, they're out to
>   prove something here. Just like we are.

                    PLUMLEY
Why you think headquarters kept
ordering you out?

                    MOORE
Just a snafu. They didn't
understand our situation.

Something like a smile passes between the two men.

                    MOORE
What are you gonna do when this is
over?

                    PLUMLEY
I ain't thought about it, Sir.
Don't reckon I need to. Cause if I
die tomorrow, fighting this way,
with you and these men, that'll be
okay with me. But I do want to go
home. I love West Virginia. I love
being home with my wife. I ain't
afraid of being an old soldier. I'm
afraid of being a shitty young one,
that's all I've ever been afraid of.

                    MOORE
I love my country. I love it more
than life. But back home, races
fight with each other. One man
walks past another, and lets him
bleed. Here, men die to help each
other. A man goes down, wounded,
bleeding, and every man in this unit
would risk his life to drag that
wounded buddy to help.
                    (beat)

                    MOORE (CONT'D)
          I don't know that I want to go home.
          I mean I do. I want to hold my wife
          and my children. But part of me
          thinks that's selfish, because there
          are some men here who won't come
          home. They'll give their lives
          here, before they'll let each other
          down. I think maybe this is the
          finest place I've ever been.

     Plumley understands. And so does Joe Galloway, sitting
     in the shadows.

❖ The following scene, another actual event, originally followed Scene 213, Crandall's return to Camp Holloway.

     INT. OFFICER'S CLUB - DAY

     The base has a quonset hut that serves as the Officer's
     Club; even out here, America has brought a sense of
     style to the proceedings. Moore, Crandall and Mills
     walk in. Moore has just walked off the battlefield,
     and still is filthy from the fighting.

     The place is full of officers, killing time and
     knocking back drinks. There's a BARTENDER there, a
     retired military man with an attitude.

                    CRANDALL
          We'll have...what're you drinking,
          Hal--whiskey?

                    MOORE
          Whiskey.

                    CRANDALL
          Three whiskeys.

                    BARTENDER
          You two are all right--but he can't
          drink here.

                    MOORE
          Why not?

                    BARTENDER
          You're too dirty.

He points to a sign above the bar that says all
officers must be properly attired, by order of the
General.

Moore unslings his M-16, cocks the mechanism and lays
the weapon onto the bar. Crandall and Mills sigh and
pull out their .38's. Moore says, through clenched
teeth--

                    MOORE
          You've got exactly 30 seconds to get
          some drinks on this bar or I'm going
          to clean house.

❖ Early drafts of *We Were Soldiers* included the events of the ambush at Landing Zone Albany, the battle following that at LZ X-Ray. They include a character named Captain George Forrest who does not appear in the final shooting script. The following scenes from LZ Albany were omitted from the final shooting script.

EXT. IA DRANG VALLEY - DAY

At Landing Zone X-Ray, McDade and his fresh troops have
loaded up tons of weapons collected from the dead NVA.
The last of the Hueys has lifted off, carrying them.
McDade is talking with his officers.

> MCDADE
> We've been ordered two miles west, to Landing Zone Albany. The Hueys are ferrying the captured weapons back to camp. So we walk.
>
> OFFICER
> Didn't Moore say--
>
> MCDADE
> We can't stay here, they're gonna have a B-52 strike all around this perimeter. So saddle up.

The officers move out, leading their men into the jungle.

EXT. THE MARCH - DAY

The men march through the Vietnamese Highlands. It's hot and the men are tired. McDade orders the column to take a break.

IN THE JUNGLE

NVA troops quietly cluster on either side of the resting American column.

AT THE COLUMN

McDade calls all of his officers to a grove of trees at the head of the column.

Suddenly the NVA unleash a flurry of rounds into the unsuspecting Americans. The American troops are green, exhausted, and without any guidance. They are cut down almost without resistance, nearly a hundred Americans falling in the first few seconds, caught in a classic crossfire of the NVA on both sides of the American column. The American officers dive for cover.

                    MCDADE
          What...what's happening?

                    FORREST
          Ambush!

Captain Forrest grabs his radio man and his
second-in-command.

                    FORREST (cont'd)
          Come on!

Forrest races through the ambush; bullets fly around
him, and he keeps running. He hurdles over fallen
Americans, over brush, over fallen trees, and he keeps
running. When his radio man and the lieutenant beside
him falter, he holds them up and keeps running.

The radio man is shot and falls dead. Forrest keeps
running. The lieutenant is shot dead and falls beside
Forrest. Forrest keeps running.

Forrest makes it to the very rear of the column, and
his terrified men.

                    SOLDIER
          It's Captain Forrest!

                    FORREST
          Make a perimeter! Circle up! And
          follow me!

They instantly rally.

STORYBOARDS

We Were Soldiers / 153

S*toryboards are drawings used by film directors to visualize how a scene will be shot and then communicate their vision to the crew. Before production on* We Were Soldiers *began, director Randall Wallace mapped out some of the battle scenes that would be particularly challenging to translate from the page to the screen.*

SCENE 172 - GALLOWAY TAKING PHOTOS

Below is a storyboard sequence that was created for Scene 172 in which UPI reporter Joe Galloway struggles to take photos with the battle intensifying around him. The text of the scene is included below each corresponding storyboard.

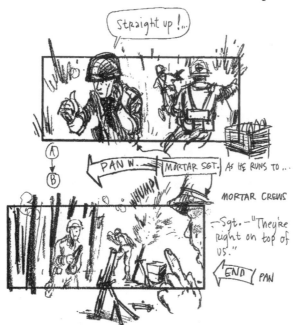

JOE GALLOWAY

lies in the middle of the landing zone, near the mortar crews who are firing furiously as their SERGEANT shouts--

          MORTAR SERGEANT
Straight up! They're right on top of us!

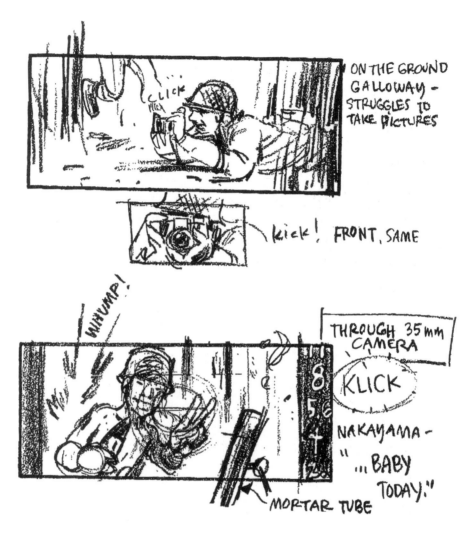

Galloway struggles to take pictures; he catches a few of a young Japanese-American, who grins at the camera even as he loads shells into the mortar tubes.

                        GALLOWAY
            What's your name?

                        NAKAYAMA
            Nakayama! I got a baby being born today!

As Galloway tries to note down the name, the man next to Nakayama is shot; as Nakayama kneels over him to try to stop the bleeding, the elephant grass comes alive, bullets skimming two feet off the ground. Galloway hugs the earth, terrified that to move anything would be to get it shot off.

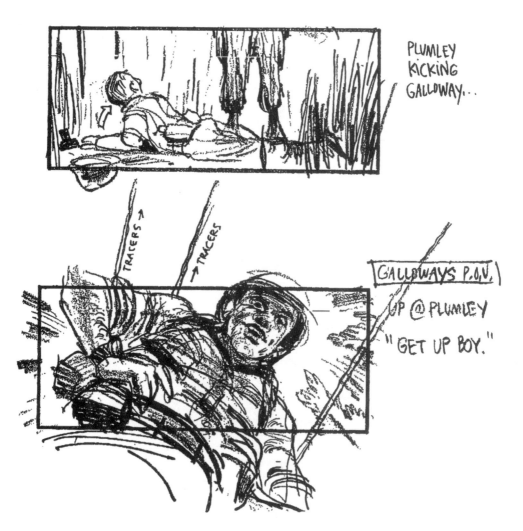

Then he feels the toe of a combat boot jammed into his ribs, and can't believe somebody is kicking him. He twists in surprise to see Sgt. Major Plumley, all 6'2" of him standing tall in the hail of gunfire.

                       PLUMLEY
You can't take no pictures laying down there on the ground, Sonny.

SCENES 2-13 MOORE'S PARACHUTE TEST

The following scene, where Hal Moore tests a faulty experimental parachute, is based on a real incident. It was never shot, however, during pre-production this complex sequence was planned in detail with storyboards.

Moore steps out of the plane.

Rake angle down plane as Moore leaps out....

EXT. THE PLANE – DAY

In its open side door stands a lean officer; he is HAL MOORE. He's wearing a helmet and parachute gear; he holds a radio.

          JUMP COORDINATOR (RADIO VOICE)
  Hang onto your rip cord, we're running
  short of 'em.

          MOORE
  Roger that.

He hands the radio to an air crewman and calmly steps out into the rush of air.

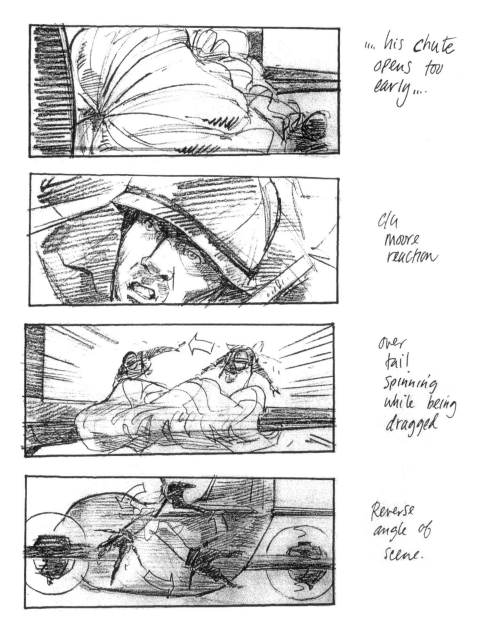

The chute snaps open too quickly; Moore's body jerks like a rag doll as wind catches the parachute silk and snatches it straight back into the huge tail section of the plane.

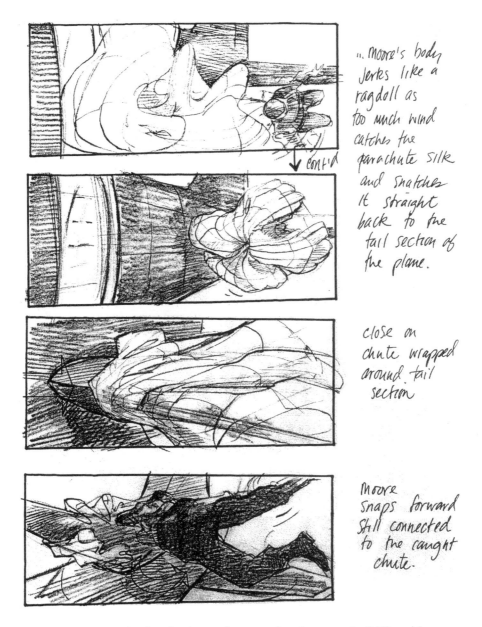

"...Moore's body jerks like a ragdoll as too much wind catches the parachute silk and snatches it straight back to the tail section of the plane.

close on chute wrapped around tail section

Moore snaps forward still connected to the caught chute.

Suddenly Moore is being dragged along at 150 miles an hour. The earth and the sky are spinning wildly for him, his chute a mess of torn silk and fouled lines.

Pilots realize a problem

Gen. Harry Kinnard raises his binoculars.

AIDE: "Sir, there's a problem"

P.O.V of plane dragging Moore.

INSIDE THE PLANE the crew reacts by hitting emergency buttons; but there's nothing in the world anyone can do to save Moore.

DOWN ON THE GROUND, THE OBSERVERS see the emergency.

> JUMP COORDINATOR
> He's hung on the tail! Maybe if he deploys his backup it'll tear him free!

> GENERAL KINNARD
> At 150 miles an hour it'll rip his body in two.

Moore's a dead man; everybody on the ground knows it.

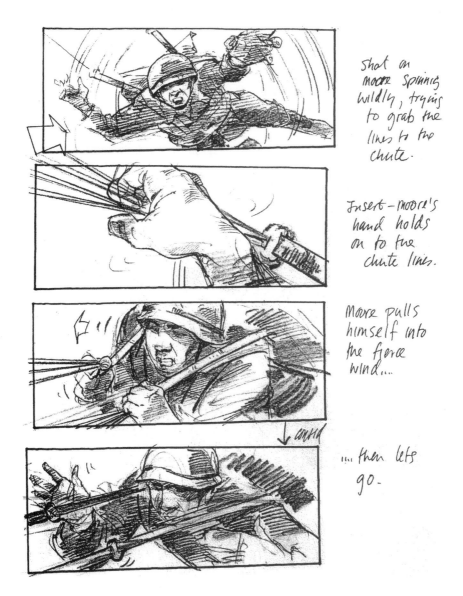

shot on Moore spinning wildly, trying to grab the lines to the chute.

Insert - Moore's hand holds on to the chute lines.

Moore pulls himself into the fierce wind....

....then lets go.

HANGING ON THE PLANE'S TAIL SECTION, AT 150 M.P.H.

In solitary, personal danger, Moore keeps his head; he grips the lines and pulls himself into the fierce wind, then lets go and the lines snap taut, but don't release.

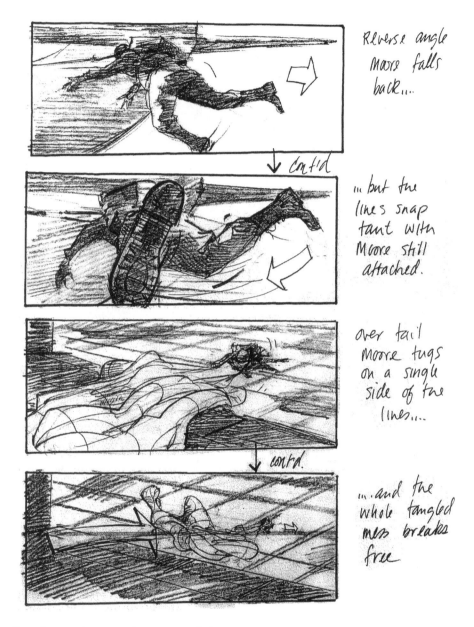

He does it again. Nothing. He tugs and snaps on a single side of the line...and the whole tangled mess breaks free.

Now he's tumbling to earth with his main chute streaming; if he pulls his reserve and it tangles in the main lines, he's dead. The earth rushes toward him at sickening speed...

ON THE GROUND, KINNARD and the others watch Moore plummeting to his death...

MOORE draws a switchblade from his boot...

...cuts the fouled lines away, and pulls the cord of his reserve.

We Were Soldiers / 167

Moore's reserve chute opens as Moore falls into cam filling frame.

cam pan to gen. kinnard's jeep

His body falls INTO CAMERA as the GROUND'S POV, when suddenly his chute pops opens, and he settles to earth.

168 / Storyboards

Moore settles to earth...

contd

...landing on a run.

Over Moore approaching Jeep

Jeep crosses frame to a stop.

He stays on his feet, landing in an easy trot, towing
in the reserve chute

Moore removes his helmet
dialogue

gen. Kinnard shakes his head and smiles

and taking off the helmet as the jeeps and ambulances of Ft. Bragg come screaming up to him. He salutes the General, hands something to the Jump Coordinator, and walks casually to a seat in another jeep.

                        MOORE
We're gonna have to lengthen the pull time.

The Jump Coordinator looks down at the two ripcords, and can't believe Moore remembered. General Kinnard shakes his head and smiles.

CORRESPONDENCE

We Were Soldiers *is a true story about the first major battle between American forces and the North Vietnamese Army. Following is the correspondence between Randall Wallace and some of the real people whose stories* We Were Soldiers *tells.*

❖ Letter from Randall Wallace to the veterans of the 7th Cavalry.

RANDALL WALLACE

To the men of the 7th Cavalry

Gentlemen,

As many of you have already heard, we are preparing to make a film version of Hal Moore and Joe Galloway's book WE WERE SOLDIERS ONCE, AND YOUNG.

I am the writer of the screenplay for the film, and also the director. Mel Gibson is set to play the lead role as Lt. Colonel Moore, and Mel's company, Icon, and mine, the Wheelhouse, are producing the film, in association with Paramount Pictures.

As you can imagine, this is an enormously ambitious undertaking. As the prologue of Hal and Joe's landmark book states, "Hollywood has gotten the story of the Vietnam veteran wrong every damn time, whetting the knives of twisted politics on the bones of our dead brothers."

Well this time, we mean to get it right.

Whether we achieve that goal will be judged by many people: a worldwide audience; a collection of film critics; our families and friends; but most of all we will be judged by you whose lives were so personally intertwined with the events of the Ia Drang Valley.

Those of us who have joined this effort view it as more than business goal; it is a dream, a mission, a holy crusade. For whatever success we achieve, there will be many people to thank; but blame for however we fall short will--and should--rest on my shoulders since I'm the director of the film and am the one who first talked Hal and Joe into letting me set out to make this movie in the first place. I accept this responsibility; I welcome it; I'm deeply proud of their trust, and I hope to earn yours.

Some of the finest film making talents in the world are involved with this production.

This film is not a documentary. The story of what happened in the Ia Drang Valley in 1965 has been documented in many ways already.

This film sets out to do what those other ways of telling your story could not: to capture the subjective experience of that war. It is not meant to tell the story of each individual, or to capture the same kind of truth a documentary would.

This is not to say that any of us making this film are unconcerned with accuracy. We are going to great lengths to capture the real experiences of you and your buddies and loved ones. The main difference in our approach and that of other media is that in movies--dramatic, as opposed to documentary, film making--we are out to communicate on an emotional level--to communicate emotional truth. Most stories of Vietnam emphasize tragic dimensions, dimensions which are true. But there is more truth than just the tragedy, and this story celebrates the truth of love and loyalty.

To tell the story of all, I must leave out the details of some. The book documents the heroism of many; the movie will focus on a few particular characters, and even those characters will be combinations of traits that existed among many characters, and many of those characters will be involved in actions that in fact involved many more individuals.

An example of this is the fact that the movie will focus on Landing Zone X-Ray. The events of LZ-Albany, its heroism and its tragedy, are alluded to, but are not the focus of the narrative of this movie.

And even withing the telling of the events of LZ X-Ray, the heroic acts of so many of you cannot be specifically detailed.

This is not because any of us lack reverence for your courage, or have any desire whatsoever to celebrate some and ignore others. It is simply the only effective way, in my judgment, to make a film that will communicate clearly and most powerfully the greater message that those who fought in Vietnam, and those who fought the emotional wars at home by loving and longing and grieving for those who fought, were heroes.

So that is our goal. From you who have already given so much, I ask more: I ask for your understanding, your faith, and your prayers.

And if you feel over-looked or slighted because your name or your particular acts of heroism are not specifically portrayed in this film, I ask your forgiveness.

But I will take what comes. I am inspired by your example, by you who gave your last full measure of courage and commitment and have lived by the light of your own example.

I salute you.

Best regards,

Randall Wallace

❖ Excerpts from a letter Hal Moore sent to Randall Wallace giving background on some of the men.

September 10, 1996

Dear Randy,

In response to your 8/26/96, this may turn out to be a partial response; we'll see.

PLUMLEY: I first met Sgt. Major Plumley the day I took command of my battalion on Kelly Hill, Ft. Benning. 29 June, 1964. I showed up very early at Bn. Hqs. to meet my Co. Cmdrs and staff before the ceremony on the small parade ground. Plumley met me at the door and we went into my small office and talked for a half hour or so.

• • • • • • • • • •

We were both about the same age. I was 42. He out of the hills of West Virginia - I from the "knobs" of Kentucky. I liked the man and his attitude immediately; laconic, thoughtful, in shape, dignity, exuded leadership, candor, good perceptive look out of his eyes, totally controlled, short haircut, strictly military. "Old-Army style" he always talked to me, in our next two years together, like "What does the Colonel want me to do about ----- ?" "If the Colonel is available I'd like to get the First Sergeants together for a talk". AND STILL DOES. He and I were both Master Parachutists - which unspokenly told each other a lot about common and similar views on aggressiveness, courage, physical conditioning, stern discipline, hard training.

• • • • • • • • • •

Every morning at Benning and in Vietnam while in Base Camp Plumley and I would get together - and later in the evening. Demands of combat sometimes prevented that. I think of a Sgt. Major like a "Sgt. General". It's very tough to rise that high.

He and I served in that battalion together in the U.S. and Vietnam for 17 months. When I was promoted and given the 3rd Brigade in Vietnam, I immediately brought Plumley up to be my Brigade Sgt. Major and Matt Dillon to be my Brigade Operations officer (he had been my Bn. Opns. officer for 17 months).

• • • • • • • • • •

GEOGHEGAN: I lost a lot of my Lts in spring, early summer of '65 as they were mostly Reserve Officers who'd served their 2 years and were discharged. I got a whole new gaggle of brand-new 2nd Lts. See p. 24. Jack Geoghegan was one of them. A gangly, red-headed, crew cut very military man. Quiet, very serious, very conscientious. I made it a point to talk one-on-one with my Lts. on occasion (I did not want to submarine the authority of their Co. Cmdrs.).

• • • • • • • • • • •

Shortly before we left An Khe Base Camp for commitment into the Plei Me - Ia Drang, my battalion had outpost line duty around a portion of the Camp. I flew in to check each platoon position and distinctly remember sitting with Jack near his foxhole/platoon CP drinking C Ration coffee out of canteen cups and talking. The next time I saw him he was dead. Plumley and I carried his body from the field.

• • • • • • • • • • •

SAVAGE: I was aware of Savage as a fine, young, 3 stripe "Buck" Sgt. rifle squad leader at Benning. After his superb performance of duty in X-Ray, Plumley and I were of course more interested in him. I saw to it that he was awarded the D.S.C. 2nd only to the M.O.H and it gives an Enlisted man another $100 a month for life.

Savage was a steady, unflappable, highly capable, never quit leader.

• • • • • • • • • • •

Randy, I will get more answers to you on your questions and the matters you raise in letters, FAXES, etc. But I remind you that our home(s) is/are open to you to visit with me (and Julie - if necessary) to discuss all this and augment all the paperwork. We can record the talks. And when in our home in Alabama we are only 40 miles from Sgt. Major Plumley, SFC Savage and other Ia Drang veterans.

More to come.

All Best —
Hal

❖ Letter from Joe Galloway to Randall Wallace on the anniversary of the battle.

15 November 1995

To: Randy
From: Joe

Last evening at 2121 hours, 30 years ago to the minute, I thought about what was in the mind of the 24-year-old kid reporter who had just bailed out of a helicopter into the tall grass of Landing Zone X-Ray. I had just beaten Pete Arnett and a team of 3 other AP guys into the biggest battle of the war. I thought of the "beat," the exclusive, the glory and had no idea I was about to cross forever the line between witness and participant.

Today, at this hour, 30 years ago, the napalm cannister exploded and I was picking up PFC Jimmy D. Nakayama whose screams rose above the din of battle. On that day, as he died, his wife's screams a world away announced the birth of his baby daughter. Today she is 30 years old.

Today, at this hour 30 years ago, in a hail of gunfire on LZ X-Ray Vincent Cantu and I held an impromptu reunion of the Class of 1959, Refugio High School. Vince called me last night, just to reach out across the years and miles to say hello, to say he loves me, to say he wanted to be with us in DC last weekend but it's too hard on a bus driver's salary when you are supporting a daughter and a grandchild.

Every November for 30 years we have all, I think, gone a little crazy. One year it caught me at a family reunion and I sought refuge in the quiet woods behind the house. As I stood there hearing the wind in the trees and listening for something else I saw my Uncle Jiggs, a bomber pilot in the Pacific in WWII, standing in the same woods. We nodded. I wondered if could hear them, too.

Thank you, Randy, for coming to meet our brothers, hear their voices, see their faces and know what is in their hearts. Thank you for what you are about to do to ensure that America will never forget these sons, will never again forget the true cost of war. We owe this to your sons, and mine, and to all of America's sons and daughters.
GarryOwen, Sir!

Joe

❖ Excerpts from a letter from Julie Moore to Randall Wallace describing her experience during the war.

June 25, 1996

Dear Randy,

    Joe and Hal have been after me to write you about my life during the time that Hal was in Vietnam and give you some background material about "my life". I tried talking into a tape recorder but hate the sound of my voice and feel so stilted, yet when I try to write something I am intimidated by the fact I am surrounded by two best selling book authors and a writer who wrote the best movie of the year! I also try to think of profound things to say but truly Randy it all boiled down to me being a "single mother" of five children, totally responsible for their health and welfare, while being scared to death for the safety of my husband. It seemed that every time I turned on the TV there was Hal describing another fight his unit had been in. Everyday I wondered would I be next to get the telegram.

• • • • • • • • • •

    I will never forget that Monday morning in Nov. '65 when I picked up the Columbus GA. Ledger off the front stoop and opened it up to Joe's story. I must have read it 10 times trying to comprehend what had happened and that name Lt. Col. Hal Moore kept jumping out at me. Somehow I got the children off to school and drove Dave's nursery school carpool. When I got home the phone started ringing and didn't quit. I totally forgot to pick up the car pool until the school called! Even Peter Jennings called to set up an interview that night with the local TV station. He wanted to film our reaction to seeing Hal on the evening news program. I did not want to do it but the Public Information Officer at Ft. Benning asked me to. I was so stunned at seeing my husband with tears in his eyes that I could hardly speak. I should have known better as the Sergeants were his brothers and the privates his sons - no one can lose that many family members and not weep. We did not make the next evenings news!

• • • • • • • • • •

    Up till then I think we thought of Vietnam as patrols and little actions that really wouldn't affect us. I stupidly thought that Hal being a Lt. Colonel he would be safely in the rear. It never entered my head that he would be up on the firing line! The Division had been on field maneuvers so much for months at a time that I really think we wives thought of it as another maneuver. We had a tight knit group of wives that really tried to help each other, took over if one got sick or needed help with the children. It is really hard to describe the special closeness that Army wives have to each other. Even though I was lucky enough to end up a General's wife, I never forgot that I started out as a lieutenant's wife and the burdens they carried of raising young children with never enough money or husband.

• • • • • • • • • •

    We tried to keep the night Hal left like any other in the family. All had dinner together, he read Ceci and Davy their evening story, finished the last minute packing. We went to bed. I tried to sleep but I just hung on to him. When he got up to leave around 1:30 a.m. I pretended to be asleep as knew I would start crying and didn't want him to worry about us. He had enough on his mind. I heard the back door shut, got up and leaned against the upstairs window and watched while the jeep pulled away in the dark - then I cried. I was 34 years old.
    I wish I could say that I was immediately inspired by a greater power to visit my wives who received those fateful telegrams, delivered by taxis at whatever hour of the day or night they arrived at the Western Union office but it was only my father's prodding that made me go. I was terrified at how I would be received - would they hate me because it was my husband who had ordered theirs into that awful place? What beautiful women they were. I told you Army wives are special. I remember Mrs Givens, so dignified and gracious. Saying she thought she had escaped the bad news and had been visiting the other wives who had received the telegrams. She received the last one delivered. The young girl who couldn't have been more than 16 or 17 totally bewildered and truly not understanding what had happened or what to do or where to go. The darling pregnant Puerto Rican girl who spoke no english (I could understand some spanish having had a Spanish maid while living in Norway) telling me how she answered the door at 3 a.m. saw the telegram, couldn't read it but knew immediately what it was and fainted dead away.

The Taxi driver banged on her neighbors door to get help for her. She later had her baby boy in the Benning hospital and we wives got a layette together for her. She then returned home to Puerto Rico. Since it was early in the War they had pride in what their husbands had done and could feel that their husbands had died "for a good cause". I thought about them so much in later years when all the demonstrations started and all the hatred spewed out. What did they have to justify their sacrifice then? I hate to fault Fort Benning about the telegrams as I think they were caught just as unprepared as all the rest of us. Benning was just not ready for LZ X-Ray - or Columbus, GA., or America either for that matter. The war in Vietnam had suddenly changed radically and violently. It was a very cruel way to tell a woman her world had just come to an end and thanks to Mrs Kinnard talking with the Fort Benning Commander that changed very quickly. The Chaplain and an officer would visit with the bad news. Course all you had to do was look out your window and see them coming up the walk and you knew! I can't really add any more to the horror those women suffered being told in such a cruel way that isn't in the book. I will never forget that tense moment when the yellow cab stopped at my door. I saw the driver get out, come up the walk. I was alone so hid behind the drapes and prayed he would go away but he kept coming. When he rang the bell I decided not to answer, that way everything would be alright. I finally said to myself come on Julie , you have to face up to what's to come so answer the door. He only wanted help in locating a house number. I literally sagged against the door jamb, white as a sheet I was so relieved. Told him to never do that to anyone again. He was so apologetic. Said all the cab drivers had really hated that duty

• • • • • • • • • • •

     I have rambled on and don't know if any of the above will help you Randy. I wish I could have made it a little more glamorous, a little more pizazz, but it was a case of day to day survival, beating back the monotony, trying to not let the children see how terrified you were over their father's safety, going to Mass every morning to get any extra help you could for him. The joy over his safe return was tempered by the knowledge of those who didn't come back. One of the hardest things to do was to go with Hal, a few days after he returned, to visit those widows and fatherless children who were still in the Columbus area. Like he has said he felt guilty that he had survived - I felt guilty that I had my husband back.

                                          Fondly,

                                        Julie

❖ Response letter from Randall Wallace to Julie Moore p. 177-179.

Dear Julie,
 This letter won't begin to say what I want it to. I know already, of the reading your letter, that I won't be able to find the words to thank you for writing it. And for more than writing it – to thank you for being who you are.
 Some people think We We Soldiers Once, And Young must be a Vietnam War story. I know – especially after reading your letter, that it isn't really about Vietnam, and it isn't really a war story. It's a love story.
 I always knew that the people who took part in that war never got the appreciation they deserved from the rest of us. But what I've learned – and know more and more, the better I know you and Hal and Joe – is that you all deserve more than our thanks. You deserve our love. I want this movie we're trying to make to do what the book does – help us know the people, know them and love them.
 But your story – so specific, so real, so plain of pizzazz, so bursting with truth and power, does that in a way that explosions and gunfire cannot do. You've told me about your heart. I know it wasn't easy to do.
 I thank you from the bottom of mine.
          Best always,
           Randy

❖ Letter from Barbara Geoghegan Johns to Randall Wallace about her late husband Jack Geoghegan.

February 15, 1999

Dear Mr. Wallace,

When I first wrote to you last September, I quoted something I had just found that Jack's mother had written. Yesterday I again found myself in the attic, sorting through a bag of old letters. I discovered six that Mom Geoghegan had written to me when Cammie and I were away for several weeks visiting family. I just have to share part of one with you, dated July 8, 1966:

"Darling, I know how you must feel about the coming weeks when men of the First Cavalry will be returning home. But remember now that wonderful face – that whole, strong, but tired body that rests so peacefully among the summer flowers and the cool green hills of St. Mary's: Jack came home months ago. Thank God we were able to see him – oh, Barbara, how many small miracles have been granted to us.

We build ourselves up with faith, submission to the will of God – and for long periods of time the structure seems secure, and then an erosion begins to penetrate our carefully buttressed stronghold – an erosion composed of any number of things – loneliness, memory, the old 'might-have-beens', the years ahead that stretch on and on, and there is no one on that road as far as we can see – no Jack – but, Darling, he is there; he is everywhere. He is in light, always in light. He is in Vietnam comforting the dying, the wounded, the scared. He is watching over you and Cammie, Dad and I. *I believe with all my soul that great spiritual things will come to people through Jack. This is a conviction with me, not just wishful thinking.*

We must rejoice for each family whose son, husband or father returns. God bless them all and God bless Charley Company - now, according to the news, the most famous company in the war - for Charley Company and the 1st Battalion, 7th Cavalry, 2nd Platoon insured the safety of a great many of these men. Oh, I know not even this can help at times and yet the whole aim of Jack's life was to get his men home. We cannot shadow the bright success of his effort with our regrets…How can we say how much we know of your thoughts? We don't have to, because we love you and each heartache of yours becomes ours."

Mr. Wallace, I highlighted and italicized that one sentence because it jumped out at me as I tearfully read Mom's beautiful words. Mom Geoghegan died almost twenty years ago. I wish she could have known how much Jack did live on in the memories of so many others in those years, especially in recent years as a result of WE WERE SOLDIERS ONCE…AND YOUNG. And I wish she could know of your efforts to carry the meaning of General Moore and Joe Galloway's book to countless others. You said in your first letter to me, "I want the film to convey the true essence of lives, the way CHARIOTS OF FIRE did for Eric Liddle." I know to whatever degree Jack may be portrayed in this film, you will capture that essence. And, as Mom said, "great spiritual things will come to people through Jack" – this time, thanks to you!

Continuing to wish you well,

Barbara Johns

❖ Letter from General Moore to the cast and crew of *We Were Soldiers*.

June 7, 2001

TO: Randall Wallace •

From: Hal Moore

Subject: Gratitude

Since the mid-80's when I was writing the first several chapters of the book, now and again the thought hit me that this book would make one helluva multi-Oscar winning movie.

Now it's happening.

Before you break up, I want to thank you and through this message each member of your miraculously organized team for the empathy and respect for the Vietnam Veteran, and for the skills you are putting into this superb production.

Back at Benning in 1964-65, I emphasized to my men that each of them in their particular duty at their level were every bit as important and necessary to mission accomplishment as I, the Battalion Commander, was in my duty at my level. The rifleman Private was just as important as I was in getting the job done; even more so when it comes down to man-to-man.

And so to all of you; Randy, Mel on down through the ranks of officials, bosses, technicians, special top directors, actors, actresses, extras, my thanks and appreciation. But I offer a very special obeisance of gratitude to the grunts, the line troopers down in the ranks who do the dog work – the cooks, the dishwashers, the guys who planted (and unplanted) the trees and the grass, the muscle men on the sets, the snack ladies, the technicians behind the scenes, the van drivers, the porta-potty and honey wagon cleaners and all the other grunts down where the rubber meets the road.

To you Randy and to your team – a proud 7th Cav salute to each of you – from top to bottom. I give all of you 7 STARS OUT OF 7!

Garry Owen!

Hal Moore

Hal Moore
Lt. Colonel, Infantry
Commanding
1st Battalion, 7th Cavalry .
LZ X-Ray, Ia Drang Valley, Vietnam. Nov. '65

STILLS

LT. COLONEL HAL MOORE

PLAYED BY

MEL GIBSON

Lt. General Hal Moore Collection

Lt. General Hal Moore Collection

JULIE MOORE

PLAYED BY

MADELEINE STOWE

MAJOR BRUCE CRANDALL

PLAYED BY

GREG KINNEAR

Lt. General Hal Moore Collection

SGT. MAJOR BASIL PLUMLEY

PLAYED BY

SAM ELLIOTT

188 / Stills

JOE GALLOWAY

PLAYED BY

BARRY PEPPER

Joseph Galloway Collection

Courtesy Barbara Geoghegan Johns

LT. JACK AND BARBARA GEOGHEGAN

PLAYED BY

CHRIS KLEIN AND KERI RUSSELL

190 / Stills

LT. COLONEL NYUGEN AN

PLAYED BY

DON DUONG

Courtesy Lt. Gen. Nguyen Hu An

A CONVERSATION WITH RANDALL WALLACE

How did you first come across the story?

I was about to take a long plane trip and wanted to have something good to read. I saw the book on the shelf at a bookstore and was captivated by its cover; the title was really poetic: *We Were Soldiers Once... and Young*. I picked it up not really knowing what it was about. I opened the book and almost immediately came across the words, 'Hollywood got it [the story of the Vietnam Veteran] wrong every damned time, whetting twisted political knives on the bones of our dead brothers.' And I knew then that I had to be part of getting the story right this time. That was eight years ago[1].

When you first met Lt. Gen. Hal Moore and Joe Galloway, the authors of the book, were they excited for you to take their story to the screen?

There was a mix of caution and enthusiasm. After I read their book, I called my agent and said, 'Look, somebody has to own the movie rights to this book so could you find out who does and just let them know I'd like to throw my hat in the ring to be the screenwriter.' And he got back to me in a short while, a day or so, and said, 'the authors won't sell the screen rights. They have been approached, but they're really not interested in selling.' So I wrote them a letter and said, 'Look, anything I say to you is just going to make me sound like one more Hollywood guy. What I would like to do is send you a couple of screenplays, examples of my work and how I approach my work. I want to make this story into a feature film and if you read my work and are interested in talking then give me a call.' I heard from them not long afterwards.

How did you turn this very technical account of a military battle into a dramatic and emotional screenplay?

It felt like a big mountain to climb, but the thing about it was that I was full of enthusiasm to climb that mountain. The book had the ring of truth, it had the grit of battle, and it filled me with a determination. It is a collection

---

1   1993

of personal anecdotes and that is precisely what makes the book immediate, real, and powerful. But it could not function as a film as a collection of anecdotes, because the anecdotes were not told in any particular chronology. So I started doing a timeline, taking the individual events of the battle and placing them in the order of where they were occurring on an absolute time scale. So my job as screenwriter was to structure the story in a coherent narrative and also to find a way to distill the essence of the battle and tell the truth of these men, of all of these men in a given narrative thread. To hopefully tell the greater truth of all the men who served valiantly in Vietnam and their families.

What qualities does the real Lt. Gen. Moore possess that make him a great film character?

I've never known anyone like Hal Moore. Since my youth I have loved to read about great warriors and great leaders in times of crisis, about their lives, what made them who they are, what their influences are. Hal is a deeply spiritual man. The code of honor that he lives by is embedded in his heart. It is part of the fabric of his spirit. He grew up in a small community in Kentucky without a lot of money, but was rich in his commitments, and his spirit and his enthusiasm. It's never wavered, and his approach to life is like his approach to war on the battlefield—one of unity, motivation, clarity and simplicity. You clearly get a sense when you are with Hal that he's positive and that he loves living, and you love living more when you are with him.

Obviously you have great respect for Lt. Gen. Moore, as well as the other real men and their families, in this story. Was it challenging to write and ultimately direct and produce a film based on the lives of real people who are still alive to hold you accountable about how their story is told?

It is certainly a double-edged sword to have the principals of a story alive and accessible. It wasn't so much that I felt an inordinate obligation to them. I did feel a sense of obligation, but I felt it in the same way I felt a sense of obligation to myself. I felt like I had become part of their world, that we were in it together; I had joined their experience. There wasn't a whole lot of choice, and there wasn't a whole lot of ambiguity about it for me. It was a tremendous inspiration more than anything else, because of who these individuals are. There are a relatively large number of men who are still alive from this battle, but primarily my contact was with Hal Moore, Joe Galloway, Julie Moore and Barbara Geoghegan Johns. These people gave me not just external information, but also internal information, of their hearts and the silences of their hearts. The courage and dignity of their lives was a direct inspiration to me.

Are moments in the script, like Sgt. Maj. Plumley's lines to Savage[2] and Joe Galloway's story about his grandparents[3], fictional or real?

In the two mentioned cases, they are not in the book, but they are real stories about the characters. As I got to know the real people, they told me more things about their lives, things that are not in the book.

The battle itself is such a huge story—what made you include so much of the wives and families throughout the screenplay?

Movies are like human beings—without a soul they are empty. A movie that lacks character is just noise and lights. Telling this story about the families at home helped me understand what was at stake in this battle. I say in my screenplay that Moore and his men fought not for flag and not for doctrine. They fought for each other. Who they were was who their families were. Who they were as people was who they loved, and we had to understand who they loved and who loved them. The stories back home were every bit as important because to tell *the* story you have to look at the whole story, and the whole story is that soldiers are human beings. They have families; they have wives and friends. There is a family relationship with each other on the battlefield, a family relationship with the whole unit.

---

2 Scenes 28 and 33
3 Scene 159

The Americans and the North Vietnamese are treated differently in this screenplay than in other Vietnam movies. Why did you choose to portray the North Vietnamese as more than a faceless enemy, and the Americans as more than drug-abusing draftees?

There are many truths about Vietnam. There are probably as many truths about Vietnam as there are people who went there. One truth that I thought had never been told was about the bravery of the American soldier. The North Vietnamese acknowledge the courage of the American soldier, so why can't we? And to me to convey what American soldiers did in Vietnam, what they did at their best, it was necessary to portray the abilities and the courage and the commitment of the men they fought against. And this story has never been a political story. Its about a fact, its about acts of courage, and to portray that you have to understand what both sides did. The book certainly recognizes and pays tribute to the men who fought on the other side of the battlefield, and it recognizes the tragedy and the death and the loss on both sides. It was essential that we recognize that in the movie.

How long did it take you to write the first draft of the screenplay and then ultimately to get the movie into theaters?

I've read about the approach that different creative personalities have taken to their work and there are two composers who for me represent the different poles of approach. Mozart is said to have conceived ideas and immediately known how every note would fall in a symphony. Beethoven, on the other hand, would write a theme and then sit down at the piano and play different variations until he had one that he liked just right. My approach to writing is more like Beethoven's. I write something, look at it, refine it, let it grow, let it develop, listen to it, and keep refining. So I wrote my initial draft of *We Were Soldiers* in a couple of months. But I always write many drafts of something before I say to anyone, "This is my first draft."

I got the screenplay into a form that was a good strong representation of the story and sent it to Mel Gibson, gave him time to react, and when he expressed his interest I sent it to the studio. In the meantime, I pulled together the key people that I wanted to work with to make the film and I also took a trip to Ft. Benning, Georgia and underwent training with the Army Rangers so that I would have the direct personal experience of being a soldier. I wanted this to be documentary-like. Not a documentary narrative, but to have the immediacy of battle, and the thrill of it, the sting of it for everyone involved. Everything included, it took about eight years to bring the story to the screen.

What about *We Were Soldiers Once… And Young* captivated you enough to spend eight years writing and making a movie about it?

I read the book in the context of everything else I had already known about Vietnam and my own personal experiences. The experience of this war was not just the battlefield experience. All Americans experienced the Vietnam War, but most of us did it remotely, through television and through all of the arguments both intellectual and emotional that followed. I have always read with a particular kind of personal interest in Vietnam. I came very close to signing up for the Marine Corps platoon leader program when I was at Duke University. Later, I thought that I would go to Vietnam as a chaplain. Ultimately, I did not go to Vietnam nor did I ever serve in the armed forces. Like many Americans I felt that I did not serve my country as well as I would have liked to. And having that perspective, I had read a lot of material about the war in Vietnam, but never a story that so personally displayed qualities of leadership and sacrifice among the American soldiers, their families, as well as the courage of the North Vietnamese soldiers.

What is the difference between adapting a book to the screen and writing a completely original screenplay?

In some ways there is no real difference in that you are creating as you go. In a book you have a reference from which to start, but with an original your reference is internally generated. But in both cases you're trying to discover a truth. You are not really handed it. You are following lights that shine within you and project forward rather than lights that lie out in the distance that you are trying to get to. So in both cases you are listening to a silent voice and following an inner light.

What is your favorite scene?

Every scene in the film is my favorite. I don't say that glibly. I loved every scene we did. I could not call "cut" or "print" until the scene was in a place where I absolutely loved it.

OTHER WHEELHOUSE BOOKS

NOVELS
The Russian Rose
So Late into the Night
Blood of the Lamb
Where Angels Watch
Braveheart
Pearl Harbor

SCREENPLAYS
Braveheart
The Man in the Iron Mask
Pearl Harbor

NON-FICTION
Gallantry In Leadership
with Lt. Gen. Hal Moore (Ret.)

Select titles available on the World Wide Web at:
http://www.TheWheelhouse.com